The Great Con

Solving the Mystery of Trump and Q Anon

Second Edition

David Lionheart

Tantuple Publishing Inc.

The Great Con: Solving the Mystery of Trump and Q Anon

 Published by Tantuple Publishing Inc., P.O. Box 1418, Driggs, Idaho 83422. Second Edition first released in October, 2021.

email: dlionheart@tantuple.com

All Scripture references are to the Authorized (King James) Version of the Holy Bible, supplemented with the names of God and Jesus from the Hebraic-Roots Version Scriptures.

Printed in the United States of America

ISBN (paperback): 978-0-9983825-2-4
ISBN: (eBook): 978-0-9983825-5-5

DEDICATION

This book is dedicated to my co-authors, YHWH (pronounced Yahuwah, the Hebrew name of God) and Yahushua (Jesus) of the Bible who inspired the words of this book.

May this work bring glory, honor and delight to YHWH and Yahushua and comfort, peace, perspective and insight to the elect in these very troubled times.

ACKNOWLEDGEMENT

I am very grateful to Luis Ortiz / Graphic Designer for helping me to design and create the cover for this book and to my friend, Michael E. Dunagin, for his able proofing and editing contributions and for his devoted friendship and loyalty.

Table of Contents

1. Introduction

On October 28, 2017 an anonymous author made this first online post to one of the 4chan boards:

Anonymous ID: BQ7V3bcW No.147012719 1
Oct 28 2017 15:44:28 (EST)

Anonymous ID: gb953qGI No.147005381
Oct 28 2017 14:33:50 (EST)
>>146981635
Hillary Clinton will be arrested between 7:45 AM - 8:30 AM EST on Monday - the morning on Oct 30, 2017.
>>147005381

HRC extradition already in motion effective yesterday with several countries in case of cross border run. Passport approved to be flagged effective 10/30 @ 12:01 am. Expect massive riots organized in defiance and others fleeing the US to occur. US M's will conduct the operation while NG activated. Proof check: Locate a NG member and ask if activated for duty 10/30 across most major cities.

Five days later, on November 2, 2017, in Post #61, this same anonymous poster first identified himself or themselves by the the letter Q. From this was born a social and political movement of millions of Q or Q Anon followers the world over who monitor the Q boards on a daily basis looking for further news and clues that reveal that the deep state global conspiracy is very real and that it had been seeking to execute a soft coup in America to oust Donald J. Trump as its duly elected President.

The principal means by which this group of secretive and criminal elements within the federal government and the mainstream media (MSM), owned and controlled by the global conspiracy and cabal, sought to achieve this result was by accusing Trump and his campaign team of colluding with the Russian government to alter the outcome of the 2016 American Presidential election. After a 22 month Special Counsel investigation conducted by former FBI Director Robert Mueller and a team of 18 highly biased anti-Trump investigators and prosecutors concluded in late March of 2019, that there was no collusion with the Russian government on the part of the Trump campaign and no obstruction of justice. In short, the entire effort to bear false witness against Trump and his campaign team had been declared, after an exhaustive investigation, totally unjustified and without merit.

As an outgrowth of what amounted to an unjustified witch hunt and false allegations for which there was no credible evidence, the chief law enforcement agencies of the United States in the form of the Federal Bureau of Investigation (FBI) and the Department of Justice (DOJ) were exposed and revealed to be lawless and rogue criminal enterprises. Furthermore, the MSM, composed of six large media conglomerates that control roughly 90% of the information sources of all media consumers, have been conclusively revealed and exposed as blatant liars who exist solely as the propaganda arms of the global elite conspiracy, that is also commonly referred to as the shadow government or the deep state. [1]

Today in February 2021, America is at a crossroads. Never in the history of our constitutional republic have we ever witnessed such blatant and public disregard for the rule of law, the unequal application of the law and a lack of adherence to the principles of the United States Constitution. For the last

---

[1] According to Google on February 10, 2021, the six media giant corporations as of September 2020 were AT&T (bought Time Warner), CBS, Comcast, Disney, News Corp. (parent company of Fox News), and Viacom.

four years of Trump's presidency, we have witnessed a series of false allegations and witch hunts against Trump that almost everyone in Washington DC appeared to be in on.

First there was the Mueller investigation by a team of 18 legal investigators who appeared to all have a distinct conflict of interest and bias against Trump that spent over $40 million and came up with effectively nothing. Next, we witnessed the circus of the nomination hearings over Trump's nomination of Brett Kavanaugh for a seat as an Associate Supreme Court Justice in which he was falsely accused of wanton sexual misconduct as a young man which proved to be groundless, but for which there were no adverse consequences borne by multiple women who bore false witness against him. Next we witnessed the sham of groundless impeachment hearings against Trump.

Immediately thereafter we witnessed the beginning of the Covid-19 scamdemic which resulted in over 40 million Americans losing their jobs and as of this date, 110,000 restaurants have closed their doors and other small businesses have been financially devastated as well. The public has been subjected to illegal and unconstitutional mandates to wear face masks and observe social distancing and sanitation practices that have been totally unwarranted for an alleged pandemic which has experienced a mere 0.24% mortality rate, no more severe than the annual flu. In the summer of 2020, a number of Democrat-controlled cities were subjected to manufactured race riots, looting and destruction of personal property and businesses designed to pit whites against blacks. Most recently, we witnessed overt, obvious and rampant voter and election fraud perpetrated during the November 3, 2020 Presidential election which the mainstream media and politicians of all stripes have deceitfully denied seeing or hearing any credible evidence of. Lawlessness, corruption and deceit are without limit today and our governments have revealed themselves to be nothing more than criminals and tyrants. These are very serious matters that have grave consequences for the survival of America as a nation and as a constitutional republic founded on the principles enumerated in the U.S. Constitution, including the Bill of Rights, the first ten amendments to the U.S. Constitution. For all intents and purposes, America as a constitutional republic is dead and our nation has been stolen in a Marxist coup without so much as a whimper.

I am an accomplished researcher, author, blogger and political, social and spiritual activist who has previously authored four rather unusual and controversial books on the subjects of the existence and workings of the global conspiracy and all its many obvious links to the recent fulfillment of end times Bible prophecy. I earned my bachelor's degree in Economics from U.C. Davis with Highest Honors and Phi Beta Kappa and Phi Kappa Phi honor society distinctions and went on to the Harvard Business School to earn my MBA degree with second year honors. I served as a systems, operations, financial and business management consultant in high tech and other related industries for over a decade and subsequently served as a turnaround Chief Financial Officer (CFO) or Chief Executive Officer (CEO) for half a dozen smaller high technology companies over nearly 20 years. As a turnaround executive, I diagnosed and healed sick cultures of troubled companies and learned how to spot and deal with the recurring issues of dysfunctional teams swiftly and decisively. I was instrumental in turning around one of those companies and selling it in a mergers and acquisition (M&A) transaction at an attractive price and turning around a second one and taking it public in an Initial Public Offering (IPO) and serving as its public company CFO for another five years.

In short, I have seen and done a lot. I have extensive first-hand knowledge and experience with those who are truly evil and those life experiences are instrumental in my ability to see things today that most people cannot. I am highly knowledgeable in economics, political science, world history, psychology and philosophy from my undergraduate studies, finance, strategy and organizational behavior from my graduate studies and biblical theology and American sociology and culture from my own independent study and all of these inform and have shaped my broad and integrated worldview today.

1. Introduction

As an accomplished CFO I made my mark by having superior information and the hard facts to allow me to keep my fellow executives on the up and up. I have a mind like a steel trap and I am highly fact-based and logical. I do not allow my emotions to influence or shape my thinking. As a strategist who understands the big picture of businesses and political and organizational systems, I think like a homicide police detective, gathering clues and seeking to formulate an integrated and coherent understanding of what all the clues and evidence are telling me. In this book, we are going to take a journey together in which we are going to gather data and analyze it together like police detectives to try to deduce what must be going on behind the scenes which we cannot directly observe.

The overall thesis of this book is quite simple, but very controversial and few people see things as I do as I am writing this. Hopefully, after I have made my case here as compellingly and convincingly as I can, you and others readers will take these insights and educate others on what the clues that are available to all of us are really telling us as to what is really going on in our nation and what is the inevitable end of all of the converging forces and developments at this most unusual of times in all of world history. I am not interested here in tickling your ears and telling you what I may think you want to hear or read. I am interested only in sharing with you the universal, objective and absolute truth, stripped clean of any wishful thinking and blind hope that is disconnected from objective reality. What you choose to do with this is entirely up to you. But I will have done my part in equipping you with the hard facts and logical reasoning that points all of us to the truth that affects us all profoundly and deeply.

Until the second edition of this book, I wrote this book using my pen name, Watchman on the Wall, for several reasons. The term Watchman on the Wall comes from the Book of Ezekiel in the Old Testament of the Bible in which God (YHWH) calls the prophet Ezekiel to serve Him as one of His watchmen on the wall, to watch for coming dangers, and if one comes, to blow the trumpet and sound the alarm of the coming calamity so that the people can prepare for the coming battle.[2] That has been God's call on my life, as I explain more fully in my previous books. So my pen name is very descriptive of my life's mission. Second, I am a fairly private and humble man. I do not like or seek the limelight and do not wish to draw attention to myself. My pen name allows me to point others to YHWH (God) and Yahushua (Christ) and for me to diminish in visibility. Third, the conclusions from much of my research have proven to be as taboo, controversial and politically incorrect as you can possibly imagine. I'm not afraid of controversy, but I do not seek rancor and a public fight either and my pen name affords me a welcome degree of anonymity and privacy. Fourth and finally, I have now authored six books and tens of thousands of blog posts and comments over the past six years under this same moniker, so using it here permits my readers to find much of my other work and connect more of the dots to other teachings of mine.

So what has changed recently that would now alter how I identify myself to my readers? Frankly speaking, my sixth book, *There is NO Virus!,* has changed everything. I believe my readers will find it so mind and life altering that I need to make my work as easy to find as possible in order to bless and benefit the widest possible audience for my books. My pen name no longer allows that. That name is now being used by several other authors which makes my work hard to find and differentiate from other people's work. That was not the case in the past. Much of my blogging remains under my pen name moniker and so I will now acknowledge both names, but my given name has no competitors, making it a bit of a no-brainer to switch to. As for the other considerations as to why I prefer to use a pen name, I will just have to deal with them as best as I can. I am fully aware that YHWH is surrounding me with a host (army) of angels guarding me from harm and that no one can touch me unless He allows it and I know He will not allow it because I delight Him and do His will completely. So I am not the least bit fearful. My

---

[2] Specifically, I am referring here to Ezekiel 3:17-21 and 33:1-11.

ultimate purpose here must be to bless as many people as I possibly can and this change will enable that objective.

I don't conceal the fact that I am a genuine biblical follower of Yahushua (Christ) and I make no apologies for it. This makes me rather unpopular in a godless world that wants nothing to do with morality, with God or the objective, absolute and universal truth. Frankly, I couldn't care less. My own life is defined by my direct, personal and intimate relationship of trust and devotion to God and to Christ, as the KJV Bible defines those attributes. I genuinely fear God, keep all His commandments and trust Him fully and without reservation. I am His faithful servant and ambassador. I read the Bible every day, I seek to become wise and I obey everything it teaches me. It is a radical way to live. In return, God showers me with amazing blessings daily. Among them, He reveals the truth to me. Many of these truths I will share with you here in this book. In fact, I am not the one writing this book; God is. I am merely taking my inspiration from Him, using the unique gifts and life experiences He has blessed me with. Watch what happens on our journey together through this book. I think you will find it rather remarkable. I certainly do. Just remember, God is talking to you through this empty and fully submitted and surrendered vessel. That is all.

You will see me quoting from the KJV Bible, where it is pertinent and necessary. In some instances, there is no other source I know of that will help me adequately explain human nature and behavior and the wisdom of the ages. You will witness me using the names YHWH and Eloah or Elohim in the place of LORD and God, respectively, and Yahushua in the place of Jesus. This is because a true relationship focuses on the beloved and not on ourselves. YHWH and Yahushua are the true Hebrew names of the Lord God and Jesus and I would be dishonoring them if I did not use the names by which they were known in the past and wish to be known today.

I hope you will consider picking up this example from me and following it in your own spiritual walk, if you choose to. And I hope you do.

David Lionheart,
aka Watchman on the Wall
Teton Valley, Idaho
February 10, 2021
Updated October 2021

2. Getting to the Heart of the Matter

Smart readers will always jump to the end of a book to discover its conclusion and then skim the intervening chapters for nuggets of insight that might help the reader determine whether he accepts or rejects the conclusions of the book's author. So, out of respect for my readers, I am going to lay out here in this second chapter exactly where we are headed and how we are going to get there. If my conclusions offend you, you might as well know it up front and not waste your time or my effort in any of the inconvenient facts and annoying logic that I intend to employ throughout this book.

Most Americans find themselves in one of two camps. One camp, the never-Trumpers, irrationally hate Trump and all he claims to stand for with unbridled passion. Most such people identify themselves with the political left and the Democrat Party and are driven almost entirely by their passions and emotions and very little by hard facts and logic. These are the people who unquestionably identify with the leadership of the Democrat Party and with all forms of the MSM and the now-discredited intelligence community (the FBI, DOJ and CIA principally).

The second camp is today made up of Trump and Q Anon fans and followers. This not a homogeneous block of citizens. Some are enthusiastic Trump supporters who dismiss Q Anon as a LARP (Live Action Role Play) and psyop (psychological operation). Others are ardent Q Anon autists who seek to find esoteric clues and to use ciphers of gematria and other techniques to deduce seemingly hidden meanings within Q's posts. Most of these Americans identify and describe themselves as conservatives, American patriots, Republicans and often, Christians. This second group is marginally less ruled by their passions and emotions than the first group and some of them are rather enthralled by the complex ciphers and gematria that the Q Anon team employs routinely to drop their bread crumbs and cryptic clues of what Q Anon appears to be directing them to go research out for themselves and to then share with other autists or anons. This second group is often mesmerized by the slogans which Q Anon has made popular over the course of the last three plus years. These slogans of the mesmerized mob include, "The Great Awakening," "Calm before the Storm," "WWG1WGA (Where We Go One We Go All)," "MAGA (Make America Great Again)," "trust the plan," and the "Second American Revolution." Such slogans speak to people's emotions and circumvent their critical thinking and always contribute to growing crowds who are easy to manipulate and control by con men and demagogues.

I have concluded that both of these two primary blocks of Americans have been deeply deceived by the orchestrated and contrived theater that has been deliberately manufactured to lead them astray and divert their attention from the simple and obvious truth that is right before their eyes that they cannot and do not see, or they see it, but they refuse to believe or accept it. I refer to this profound and deliberate deception as The Great Con. And by con, I am referring to a massive, clever and very sophisticated con job or game employed by skillful manipulators and deceivers on both sides of a fake divide and conquer ploy that all of them are in on, to one degree or another.

Through much research and thinking about what the facts I have gathered tell us, I have concluded that Donald Trump is a masterful con man who has succeeded in deceiving just about everyone and that Q Anon is an integral tool that he and his deep state handlers have developed and deployed to keep the American patriot movement docile and compliant with his aggregate policy moves and actions while Donald Trump and his globalist deep state operatives have continued the core policies of their predecessors, while throwing a few disposable bones to Trump's political support base. The way I view it, Trump, the recent Puppet-in-Chief, was new but the puppet masters were really just a different crew from the same old cabal of Talmudic Jewish Zionists who have ruled America and the world for decades. The Trump Zionist cabal merely replaced the Bush/Obama/Clinton Zionist cabal. Nothing really changed. It was all an act and con job to hopelessly deceive the American public. And most Americans have been so deeply confused that it will take them decades to figure out that they were badly deceived and betrayed by a slick con man, Donald J. Trump.

I know that this is a hard pill to swallow for most people reading this, but hold on and please bear with me. America is a nation of liars and con men and we all have been conned for a very long time in many profound ways that few Americans still understand and have come to terms with. I have. What I have to share here with you is a tragic tale of a nation that was founded 245 years ago by a collection of very clever and devious Freemasons and con men, and it has been this way ever since. It became much worse over the last 120 years or so when this nation was taken over by the global conspiracy of Talmudic Jewish and Freemason elites, pedophiles, pedovores and Wall Street thieves. I have written extensively of the details of this hijacking of America in my previous books.

It is and it should be very upsetting emotionally for anyone encountering these troubling facts and evidence for the very first time. Social scientists and psychologists refer to the stunning emotional impact upon a person who has first been confronted with irrefutable evidence that he has been deceived and betrayed by the people and institutions he fully trusted as cognitive dissonance. It is akin to taking a blow to your head and being severely confused and disoriented by it for a while. I know. I have been through this painful ordeal myself. It was not the least bit pleasant or affirming. But I had no other choice other than to integrate this new knowledge and understanding into my understanding of how life and the world really work and discard my past beliefs which had been proven to me to be monstrous lies. My worldview had to and did change and I am far better for it today.

The 1999 movie, *The Matrix,* is a metaphor and picture of what life is really like. We are all born into a matrix of lies so pervasive and distorted, that once we have been programmed by it all, anyone who has discovered the truth and rejected the lies is regarded by the unawakened masses as mentally unstable, if not outright insane. Welcome to my world today. It is a rather lonely and challenging way to live, but a noble and virtuous calling that I heartily embrace and am at peace with. In *The Matrix*, the main character, Neo, chooses to swallow the red pill and discover the full reality of the matrix of lies he is trapped in and in the end, he succeeds. So have I. I hope some of you, with my encouragement and coaching, may choose to take this same journey and to become truly free of the matrix of lies of a world gone mad.

Yet another movie that is pertinent to this journey is the 1998 movie, *The Truman Show*, starring Jim Carrey. In it, the main character discovers that his entire life has been an elaborate television reality show in which his perception of reality has been tightly controlled and manipulated while being viewed by a television viewing audience of millions of people. In the end, the main character escapes his artificial reality and discovers how totally he has been duped by those managing everything he encounters behind the scenes and out of his awareness.

These two movies are intentional messages that the Jewish global elites of Hollywood have used to signal what they have really been orchestrating behind the scenes for centuries. They knew full well that only a few of us would grasp the greater significance of their movie creations. Most people would regard them as mere entertainment and think no more about the messaging buried within the plots of these two movies. Similarly, Fabian Socialist George Orwell's intentionally prophetic novel, *1984*, first published in 1948, depicted the dystopian world in which we find ourselves living today. These are no accidents or coincidences. As part of the twisted morality of the global elites who engage in practices of the occult, they believe that if they reveal what they are doing to the rest of us and we don't object, that it amounts to our tacit agreement and acceptance of their manipulative schemes and ploys. Anyone in their right mind, once exposed to the truths of our twisted world, would surely object and would seek to escape the psychological slavery to which we all have been subjected all our lives and begin to discover the true purpose and meaning to all of life that few are ever blessed and fortunate enough to discover. I am one of those few and it is my sincere hope to be able to share the joys of a life fully lived with you, my readers. If you have not yet seen these two movies and read Orwell's book, *1984*, I urge you to do so before continuing with this book. This background understanding will be profoundly helpful to you in making sense out of the concepts I will be sharing with you here.

Yet another response that it common to people who first discover the deception of our world gone mad is to become angry at the notion that we could have ever been so badly deceived by others for so long. In short, our pride is pricked. I am 67 years old, and as you now know, very well educated and experienced in life, and yet I didn't discover anything related to the global conspiracy until 2011, some ten years ago, when I was 57 years old. Yet my pride was not pricked. However, it quickly became apparent to me when I tried to share my newfound discoveries with others, that they were in total denial of this greater reality and could not and did not want to know about it. Perhaps this describes you too. If so, I urge you to set this book aside and read no further, for it will merely upset you and lead to nothing positive or constructive for you. Not everyone can emotionally, psychologically or spiritually handle these notions that we all have been deeply deceived, and there are distinct spiritual reasons for this.

Some of you may be wondering where all of this points and what does it all mean? That was certainly my experience and in my own case, I was bound and determined to figure out where it all led since I had been beaten up figuratively by the matrix pretty badly on multiple occasions in my family, work and church life and was bound and determined to figure out how to stop it from happening to me again. In the process, YHWH or God revealed to me that only He, Yahushua (Christ) and the KJV Bible are 100% trustworthy, reliable and true and that almost nothing else is. As I began to study what the Bible says and clearly means, it became obvious to me that the signs of the global conspiracy all around us are obvious and compelling signs that we are living in the bitter last days of end times Bible prophecy and that Christ's second coming is imminent.

If that is true, and it is, it changes everything. It means that everything that most people place value in: their money, jobs, families, country, homes, cars, vacations, academic accomplishments, status, power and fame is soon going to be burned up and thus means nothing. Instead, all that matters and that will last are the quality of our relationships: first with God (YHWH) and Yahushua, and second with other people in our lives and the quality of our characters. Thus, the matrix is a construct and an illusion which God Himself has created to deceive the whole world, and then to the few whom He has chosen as His own, He reveals the truth that really matters and that He has revealed to me, some of which I will try to share with you at the end of this book, to put everything into its proper perspective.

Now that you know where we are going, it is important that we all have a common understanding of a number of aspects of how our nation and world really work, that are not how we have been told and taught that they work. This knowledge is the sort of knowledge and understanding that we must rely on to enable us to deduce what is really going on behind the scenes that we have been badly lied to about all our lives. Many of these ideas are controversial, unpopular and even taboo, to keep you from discovering them, but they are vitally important for us to understand as we examine the objective and verifiable circumstantial clues and facts of Trump and the Q Anon phenomenon.

3. Lies of the Matrix we Have Been Told and Taught all our Lives

All of us grow up operating on the assumption that we live in a world that is fundamentally trustworthy and in a nation that is fundamentally safe. But the objective truth is the exact opposite of this, as I hope to prove conclusively in this chapter. You may never have encountered many of these notions because in reality, our society and information sources are so tightly controlled and manipulated to keep all of us in the dark. The reason this discussion is so vitally important is because if you know what is objectively true, you will be able to quickly spot the liars, the counterfeits and lies and know what you are dealing with. Without this framework, truth and lies seem equally plausible and in our world ruled by Satan, the father of lies, the truth is actively silenced and suppressed and the lies are actively promoted as the truth. The reason lies are so harmful is because,

> *"A lying tongue hateth those that are afflicted by it; and a flattering mouth worketh ruin."* Proverbs 26:28

Here are sixteen of the most harmful lies that are commonly taught in America today:

1. All men are created equal.

2. All men are endowed by their creator with certain inalienable rights; that among these are life, liberty and the pursuit of happiness.

3. Those claiming to be Jews are who and what they claim to be: God's chosen people, beyond moral reproach who have been unfairly persecuted by non-Jews without cause throughout the centuries.

4. Six million Jews were exterminated by the Germans in concentration camps and mobile gassing vans from 1942 - 1945.
5. The United States federal government serves we, the people, and is in fact the government of our nation.
6. The mainstream media (MSM) exists to report the news honestly and without bias.
7. The notion that the world and our nation are ruled by a global elite conspiracy is pure fiction and is only believed by a small minority of tin foil hat conspiracy theorists and nuts.
8. Most politicians are honest public servants.
9. Political elections in America are generally conducted with honesty, transparency and integrity and the results are fundamentally trustworthy.
10. America is a nation devoted to serving the God of the Bible and is largely a moral and selfless nation.
11. The official narrative of 9/11 is trustworthy and true.
12. Those who claim to be Christians are who and what they claim to be.
13. The earth is a spinning globe that orbits the sun.
14. America put a man on the moon.
15. Man evolved from single cell organisms over the last 4.6 billion years.
16. Man-made global warming poses a dire threat to all of life on earth.

Regardless of who you are and how much you know, it is a good bet that almost everyone reading this list believes that well over half of these claims are true. Yet the simple, objective truth is that not a single one of these claims is objectively true. I intend to reveal to you here in this chapter why each one of these claims has to be false, but before I do so, stop for a moment and consider this. What if all of these truth claims are proven to be lies? If they are proven to be lies, what does that tell you about the society, culture and nation in which we live? It ought to tell you that our social, political and economic systems, institutions and leaders have no integrity, honesty or trustworthiness to them at all! And if that is true, then almost everything is fake and almost everything is a con. Let the implications of these tentative conclusions sink in for a bit. Because the ramifications of this conclusion ought to be very disturbing to all but the mentally and criminally insane. Sadly, the vast majority of humanity today is fairly described by this last statement. This should be very disconcerting to all of us. The fact that it is not disconcerting to all but a very few of us, ought to be even more disconcerting and disheartening!

Now let's examine and demolish each one of these sixteen preposterous and damaging lies and expose the truth on each one:

1. All men are created equal.

In truth, we all know this assertion to be false, even though Thomas Jefferson wrote it and claimed it in his political document, the Declaration of Independence of July 4, 1776. All of us are born with different talents and limitations, in different financial circumstances, to parents with distinctly different strengths and weaknesses, with different health, all of which are totally out of our control. Thus, the truth is that none of us are equal or the same as anyone else. And this is by God's intentional design.

What is most telling of all is how those who number among the "establishment" of the global elite view themselves relative to us. They believe that only they are properly equipped to rule over the rest of us and make decisions for the greater common good. Those who profess themselves to be Jewish (they really aren't) refer to all non-Jews as "goyim," meaning cattle, and think of us as lower than dogs.

But when it suits them, these same thought police and psychological and social manipulators assert that women and children ought to have the same rights, deference and respect as men, whose role in any healthy and functional society is to serve as the providers, protectors, teachers and leaders of their families and of society at large. But if your goal is to create chaos, anarchy and disruption in any society, in order to destroy it and take it over, as is the goal of the (largely Jewish) global elites, one way to do it is to reverse the roles of the two genders in that society to wreak havoc in families and among the two genders. This is precisely what we are witnessing in America today. Men, who bear the greatest responsibilities for passing on wisdom, morality and godly character to the next generation, are disrespected and dishonored by women and children, to the very real harm of all of us.

2. All men are endowed by their creator with certain inalienable rights; that among these are life, liberty and the pursuit of happiness.

Nowhere in the KJV Bible does God refer to the rights of man. The Bible speaks of our responsibilities to our fellow man, but rights are entitlements that almost always come at someone else's expense. Nowhere does God guarantee any of us with anything. God has created man for His good pleasure; not the other way around. These words regarding man's inalienable rights are derived from the philosophy and writings of Englishman John Locke, an Enlightenment era political thinker and philosopher with whom Thomas Jefferson was quite familiar and in agreement, and he used Locke's ideas as a tool for his political document, the Declaration of Independence. As such, it was an instrument he used to gather the support of American colonialists. It had nothing to do with the objective, absolute and universal truth; nor does it today.

Notably, the Bible teaches that God is concerned not the least bit with man's happiness, but far more with his holiness, righteousness and wisdom. All three of those attributes of good and noble character are sorely lacking in America today and we all know it, or should know it.

3. Those claiming to be Jews are who and what they claim to be: God's chosen people, beyond moral reproach who have been unfairly persecuted by non-Jews without cause throughout the centuries.

Sadly, nothing could be further from the truth compared to what is stated here. Those claiming to be Jews today (many of them being establishment elites) are pathological liars and impostors posing as what they are not. According to authors Texe Marrs and Arthur Koestler, over 95% of those claiming to be Jews today are Turko-Mongolian Khazars (commonly referred to as Ashkenazi Jews) whose ancestors converted from pagan phallic worship (something they still secretly engage in today) to Talmudic Judaism for reasons of political expediency in 740 A.D.[3] These same people have falsely claimed since then that they are the Jews, Hebrews, Israelites and Semites of the Bible and the heirs of the promises God made to Abraham, Isaac and Jacob. This too is a blatant lie. The promises God made to Abraham, Isaac and Jacob, beginning in Chapter 12 of the Book of Genesis, pertain to the spiritual heirs of Abraham, those having the faith of Abraham, namely those who were or are God's born again elect followers of Yahushua or Christ:

> *"Now to Abraham and his seed were the promises made. He saith not, And to seeds, as of many; but as of one, and to thy seed, which is Christ (the Messiah)."* Galatians 3:16
>
> *"And if ye be Christ's (the Messiah's), then are ye Abraham's seed and heirs according to the promise."* Galatians 3:29

The teachings of the Babylonian Talmud, the holy book of orthodox Judaism is, in truth, the most deceitful, hateful, racist, bigoted, anti-Christ and anti-Christian teachings the world has ever known. It teaches that Yeshu (Yahushua) was the bastard son of a whore (Miriam, aka Mary) who sits today in a boiling vat of human excrement and semen in hell for his alleged

[3] Koestler, Arthur. *The Thirteenth Tribe.* 1976 and Marrs, Texe. *DNA Science and the Jewish Bloodline.* 2013.

blasphemy. Does this sound like a religion of moral purity and holiness, or is it the exact opposite of this? The answer is painfully obvious to anyone who is even slightly honest and who is capable of thinking and reasoning critically, logically and morally.

In Appendix D of my book, M*aking Sense Out of a World Gone Mad,* I document 200 instances over the past 2,000 years in which the impostors posing as Jews have been expelled from their host countries, principalities or cities for evil, immoral, seditious, predatory and parasitic behaviors that were undermining the safety and peace of their more moral host cultures. Talmudic Judaism is not the subject of unjust and unwarranted persecution over the centuries. It is a demonic cult of extortion, murder and depravity that has repeatedly and consistently brought pain and suffering to every host culture which has let them live within their midst and which has been met by justifiable anger and outrage by their hosts.

When I assert that Talmudic Judaism is a demonic cult, I am not the least bit engaging in hyperbole. Let's permit one of their own to tell us in his own words:

> "We Jews do not like to admit it, but our god is Lucifer... We are his chosen people." -- Harold Rosenthal from *The Hidden Tyranny* (1976).

Thirty days after Rosenthal gave the interview in which he made this statement, he was murdered for it. So the god of Judaism is Lucifer, aka Satan, aka the devil. This is not the least bit in doubt and is easily verified and corroborated by other sources for those who have the least bit of interest in confirming this.

Here's what the Bible has to say about this religious cult:

> *". . . I know the blasphemy of them which say they are Jews, and are not,* ***but are the synagogue of Satan.****"* Revelation 2:9

> *"Behold,* ***I will make them of the synagogue of Satan, which say they are Jews, and are not, but***

***do lie**, behold, I will make them to come and worship before thy feet, and to know that I have loved thee."* Revelation 3:9

These disclosures concerning who the impostors posing as Jews really are have profound ramifications for America today, which has been infiltrated, corrupted and hijacked by Talmudic Jews and Freemasons over the past 120 years. In late 2020, You Tube removed my YouTube account to silence me for my similar teachings and comments I have posted in reply to numerous YouTube videos. This global elite conspiracy of Talmudic Jews, Freemasons and the Illuminati is symbolized by the first beast and Antichrist of Revelation 13 and elsewhere. There are roughly 15 million impostors posing as Jews worldwide, with roughly 6 million living in America, 6 million in Israel and another 3 million scattered around the world, mainly in positions of great wealth, power and influence, much of which they have acquired through practices of the occult, witchcraft, and cheating and stealing, which they will almost never admit to.

In America, the MSM is controlled by six media conglomerates all owned and managed by impostors posing as Jews. AIPAC, the American Israel Public Affairs Committee, is the largest and most influential political lobby in America, more powerful than all other lobbyist organizations combined, which fully owns and controls every Congressional leader from both arms of our one party political system in Washington D.C. The Federal Reserve Bank, Wall Street, Hollywood, the pharmaceutical industry, media, publishing and the military industrial complex that benefits from America's aggressive imperialism around the world, are all dominated by Ashkenazi Jews. These facts are easily verified by Googling for it on the internet. And yet there is some sort of spell or curse of witchcraft that has been cast upon the vast majority of Americans which prevents them from daring to ever question these simple facts of Jewish domination of our nation and society.

It is no secret that anyone who dares to question America's Jewish domination is instantly slandered, defamed and intimidated into silence by accusing them of the dreaded curse of being "anti-Semitic." The practice itself is totally absurd, inasmuch as most Jews have little or no Semite blood in them and what Semitic DNA they do have comes from intermarriage with whites who are true Semites and the true descendants of the 12 Hebrew tribes of Abraham, Isaac and Jacob.[4] This demographic history of the Hebrew people was well known in America and Britain 100 years ago, but since that time the Jewish global elite conspiracy has removed and destroyed most of the books in public libraries documenting these facts in a similar fashion to what is described concerning the Ministry of Truth in Fabian Socialist George Orwell's dystopian and eerily prophetic novel, *1984*.

I myself have been censored and banned from making posts on Facebook 23 times for a total of 617 days since early 2016 for revealing just who the Jews really are and the seditious acts they have engaged in during the last 120 years. Similarly, I have been permanently banned from 18 alternative media controlled opposition websites for posting similar truths there, including World Net Daily and Breitbart News. It has not intimidated me in the least. I keep on posting and teaching the truth and standing up to the Jewish abuse of power however I can, knowing that in the end, truth will win out over their evil intent and lies.

4. Six million Jews were exterminated by the Germans in concentration camps and mobile gassing vans from 1942 - 1945.

The lie of the holohoax is one of the most pernicious lies ever told and has done untold injustice to the German people for a crime they did not commit. There are numerous books which have documented the inconvenient facts surrounding this vicious fraud, conjured up by the devil-worshipping Jews to draw the world's attention away from much greater atrocities committed by Jewish Bolsheviks and Jewish-inspired

---

[4] Balacius, Robert Alan. *Uncovering the Mysteries of Your Hidden Inheritance.* 2001 and Weiland, Ted R. *God's Covenant People: Yesterday, Today and Forever.* 1994

Communists in the 20th century and to evoke the sympathy and pity of the world for the plight of the (fake) Jews as an unjustly persecuted racial minority, which Talmudic Judaism is not, as I just proved above.

The World Almanac and Book of Facts reported in its 1934 edition that there were 15.6 million Jews worldwide that year and in 1945, this same source reported that there were 15.2 million Jews worldwide, or a reduction of 400,000 over that eleven year period, during which the holohoax was alleged to have occurred. So where did the 6 million Jews who were alleged to have been homicidally gassed by the Germans from 1942 - 1945 disappear to? No one offers any explanation for that inconvenient fact other than to question the accuracy of the numbers reported by this source.[5]

The Jews who lived in Europe at that time have been classified as "holocaust survivors" and have received generous reparations payments from the German government to the tune of some $70 billion to date, which continue to this day. Moreover, anyone within the Jewish community who dares to speak up and admit that they witnessed nothing indicating such a massive homicidal act, as falsely claimed, could expect to have been severely punished for it, including being murdered for it. This is how the Jewish rabbis ensure blind obedience and submission to the Jewish false narratives, no matter how preposterous they may be.

A number of German officers and former soldiers were hideously tortured by having their testicles crushed by pliers to extract confessions from them supporting the holohoax fraud. Such confessions extracted via torture are inadmissible in any legitimate court of law, but the Nuremburg Trials, where the claims of the holohoax first surfaced, were in no way legitimate court proceedings. It was the Jewish victors' revenge being

---

[5] Clèraubat, Brian Alois. *A Greater "Miracle" Than the Lost Ten Tribes Discovered . . . – The Dead "SIX MILLION" Uncovered. . . !* 2007. pp. 196-197.

exacted on the losers of WWII, in complete disregard for international law and human decency.

Many people ask whether the tattoos on concentration camp prisoners' arms were real. They very well may have been, yet that proves nothing concerning the claims of the holohoax. Likewise, many people claim they know people who were prisoners of war in the German concentration camps. That may be true as well, but proves nothing. The Jews of the Babylonian Talmud are universally demon-possessed psychopaths and pathological liars. Their entire religion of devil worship is rooted in endless lies. They are not the least bit who and what they claim to be, so why it is so difficult to grasp that the Khazar Jews had much to gain by perpetrating the lie of the holohoax and much to lose if it ever becomes widely known and officially acknowledged that it is a hideous lie and nothing more?

The Zionist Ashkenazi Jewish Rothschilds and their followers of the rogue terrorist state of (fake) Israel used the lie of the holohoax to prey upon the sympathies and pity of the peoples and nations of the world as a pretext to allow them to steal the land of Palestine from the Palestinians under false pretenses. Without that preposterous lie, the Rothschilds and their allies would have had a much harder time creating the (fake) Jewish state in 1947 and 1948 through the auspices of the UN, a front group for the Jewish New World Order scheme. During this same time, Jewish terrorists and the regular army drove some 700,000 Palestinians from their homes and villages in the dead of night that created the Palestinian refugee problem that exists to this day, that is well documented in Ilan Pappe's 2010 book, *The Ethnic Cleansing of Palestine.* In the last several years, we witnessed Donald Trump fully aiding the rogue terrorist state of Israel to deny the Palestinians their own independent state of Palestine in what was formerly the Palestinian Mandate under the British until shortly after the end of WWII. So the deception and crimes against humanity continued at the hands of President Trump, as with all prior American Presidents since 32nd degree Freemason, Harry Truman, fell over himself to be the first world leader to recognize the illegally created Jewish state in 1948.

5. Our United States federal government serves us, the people, and is in fact the government of our nation.

In 1871, the government of the United States of America declared bankruptcy as a result of the debts it had incurred during the Civil War which it was unable to repay. At that time, a corporation entitled THE UNITED STATES was incorporated in the District of Columbia and issued stock which is held today by the City of London and the Vatican. In 1933, the government of the United States of America declared bankruptcy yet again, and as a condition of relinquishing itself from bankruptcy, American citizens and their productive labor were pledged as collateral for future debt in the form of our birth certificates which operate like security instruments on a financial exchange market that operates outside of public view.

The various agencies which are purported to make up our federal government and the 50 state entities purported to be state governments accountable to their citizens are in reality, separate corporations as well, accountable to their respective boards of directors and stockholders. Thus, the notion that what purports to be our federal government serves we, the people, is a total sham and deliberate fraud. The MSM and our schools have been lying to us for the last 150 years about how our government really works and whose interests it really serves. In truth, THE UNITED STATES is a corporation owned and controlled by bankers in the city of London and the Vatican and most Americans have no clue that this is the case; and no politician who poses as an actor and front man for this fraud is ever going to admit to it.[6] The fact that the powers that be have been able to keep all of this reality hidden from us for so long is beyond appalling and reveals just how dishonest and cowardly most Americans in any position of power and influence are today. They are all liars and all deserve

6 https://www.nationallibertyalliance.org/two-us-constitutions

to hang for their treasonous silence in the face of this massive fraud.

Now ask yourself, if this is true, and it is, and is easily verified, how could Donald Trump claim that he aimed to Make America Great Again? Is that, in and of itself, in light of this greater and hidden reality, a total sham? Of course it is!

6. The mainstream media (MSM) exists to report the news honestly and without bias.

The MSM has fully exposed itself as the propaganda arm of the CIA's Operation Mockingbird, with absolutely no interest in the truth, in connection with the obviously false and patently ridiculous Trump-Russia collusion hoax for over two years, the fake impeachment that went nowhere, the Covid hoax and fraud, the manufactured race riots, burning and looting of businesses in the summer of 2020, the monstrous voter and election fraud of the 2020 Presidential election, and currently, the second desperate attempt to impeach Trump in mid-February 2021 (which is not constitutional if he is no longer in office). This is not anything new. Since early in world history, rulers and the elites have used lies to keep their subjects in the dark regarding what is really going on in their countries to make it easy to manipulate and control the masses through deception.

Today, there are six major media conglomerates which control 90% of the information which Americans receive, and virtually all of it is deliberately false or misleading.[7] In 1983, 50 corporations controlled 90% of the media consumed in America; so there has been considerable consolidation of the media industry since then. Furthermore, every one of the six conglomerates are controlled by Ashkenazi (Khazar) Talmudic Jews and this is no accident.

Lest you think this is a new phenomenon, listen to what newspaper publisher and New York Times chief editor John

---

7 https://www.businessinsider.com/these-6-corporations-control-90-of-the-media-in-america-2012-6

Swinton openly shared and admitted to in 1880 when he was being honored at a banquet of the so-called independent press:

> "There is no such thing in America as an independent press, unless it is in the country towns. You know it and I know it. There is not one of you who dares to write his honest opinions, and if you did you know beforehand that it would never appear in print.
>
> I am paid $150.00 a week for keeping my honest opinions out of the paper I am connected with -- others of you are paid similar salaries for similar things -- and any of you who would be so foolish as to write his honest opinions would be out on the streets looking for another job.
>
> **The business of the New York journalist is to destroy the truth, to lie outright, to pervert, to vilify, to fawn at the feet of Mammon, and to sell his race and his country for his daily bread.**
>
> You know this and I know it, and what folly is this to be toasting an "Independent Press." We are the tools and vassals of rich men behind the scenes. We are the jumping-jacks; they pull the strings and we dance. Our talents, our possibilities and our lives are all the property of other men. We are intellectual prostitutes." [8]

This shocking statement was made by someone in a position to know how the media really worked 140 years ago. Given the significant concentration of control of the media since then, it hardly takes a rocket scientist to deduce that if anything, the deceit of today's media has to be much worse today than it was when Swinton uttered this shocking statement. It is a damning statement on the deceitfulness of man and his lust for money and power. This really should not surprise anyone. After all,

---

[8] http://nomadicpolitics.blogspot.com/2014/04/nyt-editor-john-swinton-and-truth-about.html

the prophet Jeremiah spoke the truth plainly in Jeremiah 17:9 when he wrote these words inspired by God:

> *"The heart is deceitful above all things, and desperately wicked: who can know it?"*

In short, all men are liars, apart from God. It is a rare man today who consistently manifests honesty and intellectual integrity in a world of endless deceit and fraud. It is no accident or coincidence that I happen to be one of those rare few. Otherwise, my authoring this book would just be another fraud and lie.

7. The notion that the world and our nation are ruled by a global elite conspiracy is pure fiction and is only believed by a small minority of tin foil hat conspiracy theorists and nuts.

Since Donald Trump's declared election on November 8, 2016 and the appearance of Q Anon on the internet in late October 2017, and the revelations of rampant lawlessness and criminality at the top levels of the FBI and the DOJ in the past four years, tens of millions of Americans are now awake to the reality that our world and nation are run by a group of shadowy characters, hiding in the background, who pull all the strings of wealth and power outside of the public's view in pursuit of a nefarious plan often referred to as the New World Order (NWO). This group of rich and powerful elites are often referred to today as the establishment, the shadow government, the deep state, or the global elite cabal or conspiracy. Moreover, much has been written since the 1960s about this group of global conspirators and some of its leaders have openly admitted, in rare moments of candor, that such a global conspiracy of rich and powerful men does indeed exist, and that it exerts a huge influence on the events of today, and upon the major events of world history.

The simple fact is that men with a lust for wealth and power have colluded and conspired with one another throughout history to gain an unfair advantage over others in which deception and secrecy are absolutely essential for their plans to succeed. By definition then, any conspiracy is always conducted in secret and leaves only limited clues of its existence, aims, strategies and tactics. That does not mean that such clues cannot be ferreted out, because they often can be, but it requires extra tenacity and determination to do so. Much of my research and writing over the past eight years has been directed at understanding and exposing the global elite conspiracy that hijacked our nation and world decades ago and rules it today with an iron fist of intimidation tactics and fear mongering.

According to *Noah Webster's 1828 American Dictionary of the English Language* a conspiracy is:

> "1. A combination of men for an evil purpose; an agreement between two or more persons, to commit some crime in concert; particularly, a combination to commit treason, or excite sedition and insurrection against the government of a state; a plot; as a conspiracy against the life of a king; a conspiracy against the government."

On April 27, 1961, President John F. Kennedy delivered a speech to the American Newspaper Publishers Association at the Waldorf-Astoria Hotel in New York City on the existence and very real dangers of secret societies that were having a serious adverse impact on America and the world at that time.[9] Here is a compilation of Kennedy's key assertions in that speech:

> "The very word "secrecy" is repugnant in a free and open society; and we are as a people inherently and historically opposed to secret societies, to secret oaths and to secret proceedings... Our way of life is under attack. Those who make themselves our enemy are advancing around the globe... no war ever posed a greater threat to our security. If you are awaiting a finding of "clear and present danger," then I can only

---

[9] https://www.jfklibrary.org/archives/other-resources/john-f-kennedy-speeches/american-newspaper-publishers-9association-19610427

> say that the danger has never been more clear and its presence has never been more imminent... For we are opposed around the world by a monolithic and ruthless conspiracy that relies primarily on covert means for expanding its sphere of influence - on infiltration instead of invasion, on subversion instead of elections, on intimidation instead of free choice, on guerillas by night instead of armies by day. It is a system which has conscripted vast human and material resources into the building of a tightly knit, highly efficient machine that combines military, diplomatic, intelligence, economic, scientific and political operations. Its preparations are concealed, not published. Its mistakes are buried, not headlined. Its dissenters are silenced, not praised. No expenditure is questioned, no rumor is printed, no secret is revealed." [10]

Many people believe that this speech and JFK's stated intent to oppose the secret societies of the global conspiracy was one of several key factors that led to his assassination on November 22, 1963. I am one who shares that view.

In 1966, Georgetown University professor of history Carroll Quigley, published a 1,300 page book entitled, *Tragedy and Hope - A History of the World in our Time*, which was subsequently reviewed and summarized by W. Cleon Skousen in his 1970 book, *The Naked Capitalist.* Quigley was closely associated with a number of leaders of the global conspiracy and was granted access to their secret documents for four years in order to permit him to reveal to the world the existence and powers of the global conspiracy and to urge the peoples of the world and his readers in particular, not to waste their energies attempting to oppose what was already a fait accompli, or an accomplished fact, which no power could possibly unseat.

Other authors soon thereafter published their own books which further revealed the nature and inner workings of this global elite conspiracy of the rich and powerful. Two notable

---

[10] https://www.goodreads.com/quotes/tag/secret-societies

works in this regard were Gary Allen's 1971 book, *None Dare Call it Conspiracy* and Ralph Epperson's 1985 book, *The Unseen Hand: An Introduction to the Conspiratorial View of History*. For anyone unfamiliar with these works, I highly recommend you read them, if you are at all interested in making sense out of this world gone mad, and I mean that quite literally.

With the assassination of JFK at the hands of the CIA, the Israeli Mossad and Meyer Lansky's Jewish Mafia, as documented and circumstantially proven in Michael Collins Piper's 2017 edition of his two volume series, *Final Judgment: The Missing Link in the JFK Assassination Conspiracy*, the CIA, in concert with the Warren Commission, which was tasked to investigate the JFK assassination and issue its findings and conclusions, began to promote the notion that anyone doubting the official (and false) narrative of the Warren Commission was obsessed with a crazy "conspiracy theory," which had no basis in objective reality. That same mass conditioning, hypnosis and psychological mind control programing, done largely through the medium of television, remains in place today, in which any mention of any form of conspiracy is immediately dismissed as a lunatic fringe "conspiracy theory," in spite of the fact that many prominent leaders of the global conspiracy have openly admitted to its existence and some of its aims.

Jewish British Prime Minister Benjamin Disraeli, who was born in 1804 and died in 1881, once was quoting as having said,

> "The world is governed by very different personages from what is imagined by those who are not behind the scenes." [11]

---

[11] https://www.google.com/search?q=benjamin+disraeli+quotes&tbm=isch&source=iu&ictx=1&fir=sUkkTNdIP4V8yM%253A%252CyyfxXHm2-Ly6cM%252C_&vet=1&usg=AI4_-kRfaFzeAberREgCEbV2CcC23sChTA&sa=X&ved=2ahUKEwiiqpbV

President Woodrow Wilson, similarly once stated,

> "Since I entered politics, I have chiefly had men's views confided to me privately. Some of the biggest men in the United States, in the field of commerce and manufacture, are afraid of something. They know that there is a power somewhere so organized, so subtle, so watchful, so interlocked, so complete, so pervasive, that they better not speak above their breath when they speak in condemnation of it." [12]

President Franklin Delano Roosevelt, in a letter to Col. Edward Mandel House dated November 21, 1933 wrote,

> "The real truth of the matter is, as you and I know, that a financial element in the larger centers has owned the Government ever since the days of Andrew Jackson— and I am not wholly excepting the Administration of W.W. (Woodrow Wilson). The country is going through a repetition of Jackson's fight with the Bank of the United States — only on a far bigger and broader basis." [13]

FDR further revealed,

> "Presidents are selected, not elected."
>
> "In politics, nothing happens by accident. If it happens, you can bet it was planned that way." [14]

FBI Director J. Edgar Hoover had this to say about the global conspiracy that is far more than a mere theory:

---

xOnhAhXHJzQIHTcxA_EQ9QEwBnoECAoQBg#imgrc=sUkkTNdIP4V8yM:

[12] http://dosmosis.blogspot.com/2011/05/quote-woodrow-wilson-secret-societies.html

[13] https://en.wikiquote.org/wiki/Franklin_D._Roosevelt

[14] www.brainyquote.com/quotes/franklin_d_roosevelt_164126

> "The individual comes face-to-face with a conspiracy so monstrous he cannot believe that it exists. The American mind has not come to a realization of the evil which has been introduced into our midst. It rejects even the assumption that human creatures could espouse a philosophy which must ultimately destroy all that is good and decent." [15]

David Rockefeller, in a speech he gave before the Trilateral Commission in June of 1991, freely admitted,

> "We are grateful to the Washington Post, the New York Times, Time Magazine and other great publications whose directors have attended our meetings and respected their promises of discretion for almost 40 years. . . It would have been impossible for us to develop our plan for the world if we had been subjected to the lights of publicity during those years. But, the world is more sophisticated and prepared to march towards a world government. The super national sovereignty of an intellectual elite and world bankers is surely preferable to the national auto determination practiced in past centuries." [16]

In his book, *Memoirs*, Rockefeller wrote,

> "For more than a century ideological extremists at either end of the political spectrum have seized upon well-publicized incidents such as my encounter with Castro to attack the Rockefeller family for the inordinate influence they claim we wield over American political and economic institutions. Some even believe we are part of a secret cabal working against the best interests of the United States,

---

[15] https://cognitive-liberty.online/j-edgar-hoover-on-monstrous-conspiracy-and-morality/

[16] https://paloaltoonline.com/square/2006/07/04/read-these-nwo-quotes-from-the-real-enemies-of-the-usa

> characterizing my family and me as 'internationalists' and of conspiring with others around the world to build a more integrated global political and economic structure--one world, if you will. If that's the charge, I stand guilty, and I am proud of it." [17]

Simply put, those in a position of power to know these sorts of things have repeatedly admitted to the existence of a powerful global conspiracy as being entirely true. Those seeking to dismiss this notion as a tin-foil hat conspiracy theory have something they are desperate to hide and all they have left is to deny the obvious truth by demeaning and dismissing it as a mere theory, unsupported by any credible facts. We ought to be able to see right through their denials in light of recent national and world events. It's painfully obvious that a global conspiracy exists and that its tentacles reach into virtually every sphere of human endeavor today, and most people are terrified of it. But I am not, nor do I have a reason to be.

From my own extensive research, I have concluded that not only is the global conspiracy very real, but that its many manifestations reveal that it is the Antichrist economic and political beast system described using metaphors and symbolic language in Revelation 13:1-10 and that we are witnessing all around us the fulfillment of end times Bible prophecy right before the second coming of Yahushua must occur. I fully reveal all the evidence for this in my books, *Making Sense Out of a World Gone Mad* and *The Final Act of God's Play.*

8. Most politicians are honest public servants.

This lie has to be one of the most laughable and preposterous ones. In truth, not a single politician is the least bit honest or has any integrity. This is because all politicians are drawn to the power, money and fame which are attached to higher political office. Hence, politics attracts a class of individuals with serious character flaws in the first place. The two attributes

---

[17] https://opengov.ideascale.com/a/dtd/David-Rockefeller-s-book-Memoirs-admits-secretly-conspiring-for-a-NWO/4007-4049

common to all politicians is that 1) they lie well and get away with it, and 2) they have one or more embarrassing indiscretions in their pasts, which their globalist puppet masters know all about, which makes them easily compromised and blackmailed.

When you combine character-disordered individuals into an institution such as the U.S. Congress, you have a recipe for disaster. Anyone with the least bit of wisdom and life experience knows that bad company corrupts good character; and as I've just explained, every last one of the 435 members of the U.S. House of Representatives and the 100 members of the U.S. Senate are moral deviants to begin with. Forget about whether they have effective public relations gimmicks that conceal or deny the truth of who these people really are. When you put such people together, they will inevitably collude with one another to deceive and steal whatever they can at the public trough. Proverbs 13:20 explains that,

> *"He that walketh with wise men shall be wise: but a companion of fools shall be destroyed."*

Every last member of the U.S. Congress is a wicked fool. Don't be fooled by their fancy suits and ties and presentable appearances on the news broadcasts of the lying MSM. They are all in bed with one another; in many cases, quite literally.

Retired NYPD vice detective James (Jimmy Boots) Rothstein, who was and is an expert in human sex trafficking, has estimated that 70% of the U.S. Congress is compromised by pedophilia. And what about the other 30% who are not so compromised? They have to know, but they say and do nothing about it, likely out of fear for the physical safety of themselves and their family members. One former member of a high-level Illuminati family has estimated that 100% of the U.S. Senate and at least 90% of the U.S. House of Representatives are members of the Luciferian secret society of the Illuminati. If this is true, and I think it quite likely that it is, any hope of draining the swamp in Washington D.C. is wishful thinking and a pipe dream. Things are much worse and much more spiritually dark than most Americans can possibly imagine them to be. Moreover, the inability to grasp the depths of the spiritual darkness that grips our nation and our nation's capital are an essential element that makes it impervious to removal. Most Americans have no real clue that the true enemy they are opposing is the devil, the father of lies and the destroyer himself, to whom every politician has sold his soul long ago.

9. Political elections in America are generally conducted with honesty, transparency and integrity and the result are highly trustworthy.

Once again, nothing could be further from the truth. All elections are rigged and votes are never counted or reported accurately. A little bit of critical thinking reveals this to be true. But don't expect anyone involved in elections to ever admit it to you. They never will.

Communist and Soviet leader Joseph Stalin was once quoted as saying,

> *"It is enough that the people know there was an election. The people who cast the votes decide nothing. The people who count the votes decide everything."* [18]

Joseph Stalin never lost an election. Now connect the dots.

We know that election and voting fraud is quite common in America. The November 2018 midterm elections revealed a number of improprieties and election rigging in places like Broward County, Florida and California, two places which have a long history of election rigging and fraud. For everything we do hear about, there are likely 20 instances that we hear nothing about.

One clue that elections are rigged is FOX News reporting of the California midterm elections in 2018 in which FOX called the results of a number of California races 90 minutes before the polls closed in those voting precincts. Clearly, the lying

---

[18] https://www.brainyquote.com/quotes/joseph_stalin_109571

MSM had been supplied with a script they were instructed to use to inform the voters of who the globalists had selected to be declared the winner of each election contest before voting day. What is incredible here is that no one ever seems to rat on the rigged electioneering. Part of it may be explained by the fear of what may happen to anyone who dares to become a whistleblower, but it is likely that more of it is explained away by rampant apathy and dishonesty of America's selfish, dishonest and apathetic culture.

Two months after the November, 2020 Presidential election, we witnessed the alternative news on the internet, Newsmax TV and One America News Network (OAN) report that rampant ballot stuffing and electronic voting machine manipulations were witnessed and attested to in hundreds of affidavits signed by first hand witnesses of the November 3, 2020 Presidential election. Meanwhile the mainstream media (MSM), with a single voice, repeated endlessly the obvious lie that no one has produced any evidence of material voting or election counting irregularities and took it upon themselves, well exceeding their rightful role in this process, to declare Joe Biden and Kamala Harris as the winning team. Then, on January 6, 2021, the U.S. Congress certified the rigged Electoral College votes as legitimate and constitutional, when they clearly were neither. Clearly, someone had been lying in a monstrous and criminal way for two months, while attorneys working with or on behalf of the Trump campaign filed legal briefs and lawsuits in Pennsylvania, Georgia, Michigan, Arizona, Nevada and Wisconsin. As-yet-unproven claims are swirling on the internet as I write this, that Trump may have won as many as 410 electoral votes in a landslide victory over Joe Biden and these claims appear to be quite credible. If any of these claims are proven even remotely true, the Democrat Party and all of the mainstream media will be exposed and proven as the treasonous criminals and election thieves that they are being accused of by the Trump campaign and their allies today. It is hard for me to imagine that the Democrat Party and the colluding and treasonous mainstream media will survive this exposure and open public shame and that they deserve to be permanently shut down as the organized criminal enterprises they clearly are and have been.

America as a nation and empire is effectively through, barring some form of divine intervention, which I believe may indeed occur at some point in the near future.

10. America is a nation devoted to serving the God of the Bible and is a moral and selfless nation.

This blatant lie doesn't even pass the smell test of reasonableness in 2021. YHWH, the God of the Bible, is a God of truth. America is a nation made up primarily of pathological liars, frauds and con artists who are in the service of the devil, the father of lies and the destroyer. Nowhere is this more evident than it is inside all forms of organized religion, all of which are, and always have been, demonic con jobs of the devil. They lie and practice the exact opposite of what the Bible clearly says and means. Many pastors, ministers and priests are Freemasons. Freemasonry is Satan worship in disguise and a total fraud.

Anyone who bothers to do the research knows that our nation's capital, Washington D.C., was designed in accordance with architectural principles of Freemasonry and the occult. The Washington Monument, a 555 foot tall obelisk that is buried 111 feet deep, thus totaling 666 feet in total length (see Revelation 13:18), signifies the shaft of Baal in the occult. The shadow it casts as the sun rises in the east and sets in the west symbolically impregnates many of the major landmarks of our federal government, including the Lincoln Memorial in the west, the White House to the north and the Capitol Building with its dome in the east. The dome of the Capitol Building symbolizes a womb, which is quite fitting for the sex cult of Freemasonry that has this nation in its death grip of endless deception and perversion.

Two notable proofs that our American culture has gone totally demonic are the over 60 million abortions that have been performed in America since the 1973 Supreme Court ruling of Roe v. Wade that legalized the murder of the unborn in the womb, serving as a massive human blood and child sacrifice, and the public sanctioning of same sex marriage in June 2015, which fulfills the prophecy of the abomination that causes desolation (of the human race if taken to its extreme) of Matthew 24:15, standing in the place of holy matrimony between one man and one woman for life. America is one spiritually dark and sick nation and for anyone to claim that we are one nation under God makes a mockery of such a notion. America's god is Satan. That much is a virtual certainty and the fact that anyone would get offended by my pointing out this obvious fact reveals just how far we have fallen morally and spiritually as a nation.

<u>11. The official narrative of 9/11 is trustworthy and true.</u>

By now, you have to know where I am going on this. A little honest research on anyone's part will reveal that the attack on the world trade center towers in New York City on 9/11 was an inside job and false flag attack perpetrated upon America by the rogue terrorist state of (fake) Israel, aided and abetted by top federal government officials, in blatant collusion and complicity with the lying mainstream media.[19] [20] Anyone who is not enraged by this crime against humanity perpetrated by the demon-possessed psychopaths and pathological liars posing as our leaders is a wicked fool bound for hell. There is no nice way to say this. Nor should there be. Nothing about this travesty and horror is the least bit noble or nice.

Now look at all public officials and media pundits, none of whom dare to expose this rampant fraud for what it so clearly is, and we all know it to be that. They keep promoting the vicious lie and we all go along with it or seethe in rage at the evil they and their demonic lies represent that they continue to foist on those of us who know the truth. What politician or media talking head has dared to say a thing about this

---

[19] Hendrie, Edward. *9/11 Enemies Foreign and Domestic: Secret Evidence Censored from the Official Record Proves Traitors Aided Israel in Attacking the USA*. 2010

[20] Thorn, Victor. *Made in Israel: 9-11 and the Jewish Plot Against America.* 2011.

abomination? Not one! Cowardice, immorality, deceit and greed define this nation from top to bottom and Donald Trump did virtually nothing to expose this overt and collective fraud for what it so clearly is. Was he making America great again, when it never was great, but was always a Masonic fraud? No, Donald Trump perpetuated the lies and frauds of his predecessors and those claiming to be American patriots, conservatives and evangelical Christians went right along with this scam of the millennium. If God is real, and He is, Trump and America are in for a big fall!

12. Those who claim to be Christians are who and what they claim to be.

According to the Pew Research Center, there are 2.2 billion people who profess themselves to be Christians worldwide, to which I say, Hogwash! Over 99% of these people are self-deceived or knowing frauds who have no clue what it means to be a true follower of Yahushua and have no interest in the truth.

How can I say such a thing? Simple. The Bible teaches that God is the God of truth and that Yahushua is the way, the truth and the life and that no one comes to the Father (YHWH) but through Him in John 14:6. Furthermore, the devil, who is very real, is the father of lies and the destroyer. Boiling it all down to its essence, either a person fears God, keeps all His commandments, trusts Him fully and does not play fast and loose with the truth, or he doesn't. I have observed and participated in 10 different churches and para-church organizations beginning in late 2005 and ending in early 2015 and not one of them proved to have any genuine integrity, honesty and faithful adherence to living out the teachings of the the entirety of the KJV Bible from beginning to end. Moreover, in August of 2013, YHWH spoke these very words to me:

> *"All forms of organized religion are, and always have been, demonic."*

At first, this statement seemed extreme to me and for another 18 months I invested time in two more church communities.

3. Lies of the Matrix we Have Been Told and Taught all our Lives

Not surprisingly, YHWH revealed to me how right He always is once again, and I no longer have anything to do with any form of organized religion for this reason. The prophecies of 2 Thessalonians 2:3, 2 Timothy 3:1-7 and 4:3-4 have now been perfectly fulfilled; the falling away and apostasy of all forms of organized religion is complete and universal.

The vast majority of humanity have always been dishonest liars. Some are more overt about it than others, but the fact remains that most people play games and play fast and loose with the truth, especially when it comes to being obedient to all the commandments of God in the Bible. So different denominations of churches play different games of deceit with themselves, and they all claim to have exclusivity and perfection when it comes to teaching and living out faithfully what the Bible says and means. I'm telling you from my own direct and personal experience that none of them come even remotely close to doing such a thing.

Nothing is the least bit a surprise to YHWH. In fact, He orchestrates everything in all of life in accordance with His predestinated plan for His elect. It stands to reason that the devil would have figured out long ago that the best way to deceive people would be to take over all forms of Christian churches and rule and defile them by cunning schemes of deceit and fraud. And that's precisely what has happened.

How does someone with a real heart for knowing YHWH and Yahushua as they are avoid getting swept up in this massive spiritual fraud? By picking up a KJV Bible and reading it carefully from beginning to end and doing so multiple times without end. I am now on my eighth full read of the Bible, and I am deriving more and deeper insights into the thoughts and ways of YHWH and Yahushua each time I read the same passages that I have read numerous times before. As we mature spiritually and grow in godly wisdom, God reveals more of His truths to us through His supernatural book, the Bible, that can only be grasped and properly understood with YHWH's Holy Spirit of truth guiding us.

When we have a firm grasp of what the Bible says and means, 100% of which is trustworthy, reliable and true, it is quite easy to spot the counterfeits of false religion that are ubiquitous today. But without that foundational knowledge, understanding and direct, personal and intimate relationship with YHWH and Yahushua, we are easily deceived, misled and often eternally harmed.

This thought process is closely analogous to how the FBI reportedly trains its agents on how to spot counterfeit currency by putting trainees in a room with real currency which they have them handle, crinkle, hold up to the light and otherwise closely examine, so that when they encounter counterfeit currency, they instantly spot and recognize them as such. There is no other way than to do the work of mastering the truth to spot the lies, many of which sound quite credible and reasonable, until you know what the truth is.

As mentioned previously, Jeremiah 17:9 teaches us that,

> *"The heart is deceitful above all things, and desperately wicked: who can know it?"*

This is a condemnation of the nature of all of mankind. In essence, all men, apart from God, are liars and serve the devil, the father of lies and the destroyer. This is how we all are born, and it is how we all shall die, unless YHWH performs a miracle in us and places His Holy Spirit of truth in some of us that begins to transform our wicked natures into truthful and upright ones. Most of the time, He does this by subjecting us to many trials and much suffering, affliction, opposition, persecution and tribulation, much along the lines of what Yahushua suffered during His ministry on earth.

YHWH does not place His Holy Spirit of truth in just anyone. Quite the contrary; He only does this with people whom He has chosen since before the foundations of the world, and wrote their names in the Lamb's book of life, who would one day receive YHWH's Holy Spirit in them, YHWH would orchestrate events in their lives so that they would hear the full gospel preached, they would believe it, only by the power of YHWH's Holy Spirit working in and through them, and thus be saved. These chosen people are referred to as God's elect in the Bible and the process I have just described is what the term being born again (in YHWH's Holy Spirit) refers to. This almost never happens to a person who is not brought to his or her knees, broken, desperate and out of answers, first. It most assuredly is not the result of a person responding to an altar call or praying the sinner's prayer, both of which are tricks and ploys of dishonest charlatans posing as pastors, ministers, priests or evangelists. A genuine born again experience results in a radical transformation in a person's life priorities and a hunger for God's word, the Bible, to get to know God as He truly is and as He has revealed Himself to His born again elect, through His word, the KJV Bible. It is very rare today.

Here is what three prophecies that have been fulfilled perfectly in the last six or seven years predicted, that have now come true with respect to all forms of organized religion and to most of those professing themselves to be Christians, but are not:

> *"Let no man deceive you by any means: for that day (the day of the second coming of Yahushua) shall not come, except there come a falling away first (a great apostasy), and that man of sin be revealed, the son of perdition (this is a metaphor for the first beast of Revelation 13, the economic and political beast system and global conspiracy of Talmudic Judaism and Freemasonry)."* 2 Thessalonians 2:3 (Parentheticals added for clarity)

> *"This know also, that in the last days perilous times shall come. For men shall be lovers of their own selves, covetous, boasters, proud, blasphemers, disobedient to parents, unthankful, unholy. Without natural affection, trucebreakers, false accusers, incontinent, fierce, despisers of those that are good, Traitors, heady, highminded, lovers of pleasures more than lovers of God (Eloah); Having a form of godliness, but denying the power thereof: from such turn away. For of this sort are they which creep into houses, and lead captive silly women laden with sins, led away with divers lusts, Ever learning, and never able to come to the knowledge of the truth."* 2 Timothy 3:1-7

> *"For the time will come (and now is) when they will not endure sound doctrine; but after their own lusts shall they heap to themselves teachers, having itching ears; And they shall turn away their ears from the truth, and shall be turned unto fables."*
> 2 Timothy 4:3-4 (Parenthetical added for clarity)

Anyone of the truth can clearly see that we are now living in those last days and that these three fulfilled prophecies accurately describe and define our world and nation today.

13. The earth is a spinning globe that orbits the sun.

The earth is stationary and flat with a dome or firmament over it inside of which revolve the sun and the moon in a clockwise direction, when viewed from above. I know that we have all been told and taught that the earth is the third planet from the sun and that it spins on an imaginary axis that makes one full revolution per day and that the earth orbits the sun, that is purported to be 93 million miles away from earth, once a year or every 365 days. A little simple math from high school geometry ought to demonstrate to most people how utterly preposterous this notion is and has been ever since it was first advanced as Copernican heliocentrism roughly 500 years ago by the Masons, Jesuits and the Roman Catholic Church in order to try to discredit the infallibility of the Bible.

If these claims were true, then a circular orbit of the earth would require the earth to travel the circumference of a circle with a radius of 93 million miles, which equates to a diameter of 186 million miles. The formula for calculating the circumference of a circle is $\pi X d$. 3.1416 X 186,000,000 miles = 584,337,600 miles. The number of hours in a year is 365 X 24 = 8,760 hours. Dividing the number of hours into the distance to be travelled in a year is 584,337,600/8760 or 66,705 miles per hour that we would have to be hurtling around the sun for this to be true! But do we have any evidence supporting the claim that we all are living on a ball which spins at 1,040 miles per hour at the equator, while hurtling around the sun at a whopping and highly suspicious 66.7K miles per hour? No, we have no such evidence at all and if we wish to do a little research, we can quite easily prove that this has to be false. But very few people in our world today are the least bit interested in the truth or intellectual consistency, because the truth is not in them. Just in case a few of you wish to retrace my steps, I strongly encourage you to read the following books on this subject:

The Greatest Lie on Earth by Edward Hendrie,

The Earth is not Moving by Marshall Hall, and

The Flat-Earth Conspiracy by Eric Dubay

Now if this is true, and it is, it means that all the non sense we have been told about the Big Bang and space has to be part of this monstrous set of lies too. So next time you read anything about outer space and its attributes, you can be virtually certain that you are being lied to yet again. Are you angry yet? You should be.

14. America put a man on the moon.

America never put a man on the moon. Film producer Stanley Kubrick and his film crew filmed what were purported to the world to be the moon landing shots in the Nevada desert at night.[21] [22]

There are many other clues that reveal that the alleged moon landings were the biggest media hoax in history before the 9/11 false flag attack and inside job. Today, NASA spokesmen claim that they have lost the technology that allowed them to go to the moon under the NASA Apollo program which, in and of itself, is not the least bit credible. During his Presidency, Donald Trump ordered the creation of a sixth service of the military, the Space Force. In short, Trump promoted the con job and hoax that space is real, as NASA claims it is. It is not. It too is a monstrous fraud and Trump fed and promoted it.

---

[21] Shannan, Pat. *Everything They* Ever Told Me Was a Lie.* American Free Press, Washington, D.C., 2010, Section 3, starting at p. 77.

[22] https://www.youtube.com/watch?v=U0kNwvZm_9Q

15. Man evolved from single cell organisms over the last 4.6 billion years.

In 1859, Charles Darwin first published his book, *Origin of the Species*, which claimed that man evolved from single cell organisms over the last 4.6 billion years. It's what we all have been told or taught since our sophomore year high school biology classes. But is it any more true than Copernican heliocentrism and space travel? No, it is not, and it too is quite easy to debunk as the overt fraud that it is and I do so in my book, *Making Sense Out of World Gone Mad* at pages 230 - 233. In it, I reveal on page 232 that:

> "Finally, and perhaps the most damning evidence of all for the fraud of macro-evolution, the Pharisees of Zionism, in the *Protocols of the Learned Elders of Zion,* brazenly boast how easily they invented and promoted Darwinism, Communism and the godless philosophies of Friedrich Nietzsche:
>
> > *"The intellectuals of the goyim will puff themselves up with their knowledges and without any logical virification (sic) of them will put into effect all the information available from science, which our agentur specialists have cunningly pieced together for the purpose of educating their minds in the directions we want.*
> >
> > *Do not suppose for a moment that these statements are empty words:* **think carefully of the successes we arranged for Darwinism, Marxism, Nietzsche-ism**. *To us Jews, at any rate, it should be plain to see what a disintegrating importance these directives have had upon the mind of the goyim."* [23] (Boldface added for emphasis)

[23] *Protocols of the Meetings of the Learned Elders of Zion.* 1934. Protocol 2 paragraphs 3 & 4, p. 13.

16. Man-made global warming poses a dire threat to all of life on earth.

Here, once again, we are looking at a bald-faced lie. In 14 of the last 15 years, average global temperatures have been declining, not increasing. Furthermore, meteorologist and author Brian Sussman, in his book, *Climategate,* states:

> "Allow me to summarize, because I know you are going to dog-ear this page:
>
> 1. CO_2 comprises .038 percent of the earth's atmosphere, and of that amount, a mere 3 percent is generated by mankind.
> 2. CO_2 emissions created by human activity account for .116% of the greenhouse effect.
> 3. Since the end of the Little Ice Age (150 years ago) the amount of carbon dioxide has increased 35%, well within historical norms.
>
> The world is being hoodwinked. There is no planetary emergency caused by an abundance of carbon dioxide. And, even if anthropogenic CO_2 was a life-threatening issue, the earth has efficient mechanisms in place to accommodate it." [24]

Thankfully, President Trump withdrew the United States from America's continuing participation in the UN Paris Climate Accords during his first year in office in 2017. But today, we see junior Congresswoman Alexandria Ocasio-Cortez and other lying Democrat Party politicians proclaiming that the world has a mere 12 years before all life on earth is extinguished due to America's consumption of fossil fuels. In response they are promoting an insane and ludicrous Green New Deal to address a bald-faced lie and non-problem and they all know it.

Summary

[24] Sussman, Brian. *Climategate.* p. 70.

Now stand back and reflect on what we have examined together here in this chapter. To reveal and expose any one of these lies for what it is is profoundly taboo and politically incorrect today. Because this is how the world's global elites have been controlling and trying to intimidate all of us to not think logically or critically. In fact, to do such a thing today is very rare. Now combine all sixteen of these monstrous lies together and what do you have? A world that has gone mad and is totally nuts. Is it possible that this story can have a happy ending for most people alive on earth today? A critically thinking person can clearly see that such an outcome is, at best, highly unlikely. I contend that it is impossible. Something is dreadfully wrong in our world today and deep down we all know it. Only a very few of us are willing to talk openly and candidly about it. Because only then can we make sense out of that which seems to make no sense at all.

Moreover, no man, or group of people, is capable of reversing a set of conditions that govern our world today which God Himself has orchestrated over many centuries to bring us to the point we are at today. This is the compelling argument and reason why Donald Trump could not possibly have been America's last minute savior and world hero, as much as many American patriots, conservatives and Christians wishfully hoped that he might have been. In fact, as we shall soon see, he has been a symptom of what ails humanity today. It is virtually certain that God used Donald Trump to reveal to a few of us just how wicked, depraved, and slick at sin most of mankind has become at this critical time in all of world history. Much as God used Pharaoh in the days of Moses and the exodus from Egypt to reveal His awesome might and power, God used Donald Trump for much the same purpose over the past four years, in a story that has not yet fully played itself out, although it soon will.

4. The Holes in Donald Trump's Armor

The wisdom of the ages reveals that the quality of all men is revealed by their character and that a man's character is revealed by his actions and the company he keeps over a long period of time. In this chapter, we are going to examine together what some of these key principles of upright character are and examine what is publicly available information on Donald Trump to try to deduce for ourselves who he really is, and what, if anything, he was likely to do and stand for when the chips were down and he was under severe stress.

Principles of Wisdom and Upright Character

Our world today is ruled by wicked fools, as opposed to wise men of good and trustworthy character. Therefore, it is not the least bit likely for us to find a source of reliable and unchanging wisdom within our popular culture or schools. It just is not there today. In light of this sad, but undeniable situation, is there any reliable source we can turn to in times of need to discover what true wisdom and upright character looks like that never changes? And why is this the least bit important? The good news is that there is such a reliable source right underneath all of our noses. The bad news is that few people know of it and even fewer avail themselves of it. This is the root cause for why our world has gone mad today and is largely wicked and foolish. For the few of us who do pursue this timeless source of knowledge and wisdom, we can make sense of where our world is soon headed.

There is only one source of true and unchanging wisdom that I have ever found and it is YHWH or God and His teachings of the KJV Bible, especially in the Books of Proverbs and

Psalms. This is why I have been reading a chapter every night from the Book of Proverbs for over the past twelve years and have been reading half of the psalms (75 of them) from the Book of Psalms every sabbath on Saturdays for over the past five years. My goal has been to grow in wisdom, knowledge and understanding so that I might be able to easily spot the wicked and the foolish whenever they show up in my life and to know how to deal with them effectively whenever I encounter them.

So what do these books of wisdom and knowledge teach us? Here are a few verses that I have come to have an especially profound appreciation for:

> *"The fear of the LORD (YHWH) is the beginning of knowledge: but fools despise wisdom and instruction."* Proverbs 1:7
>
> *"These six things doth the LORD (YHWH) hate: yea, seven are an abomination to him: A proud look, a lying tongue, and hands that shed innocent blood, An heart that deviseth wicked imaginations, feet that be swift in running to mischief, a false witness that speaketh lies, and he that soweth discord among the brethren."* Proverbs 6:16-19
>
> *"Reprove not a scorner, lest he hate thee: rebuke a wise man, and he will love thee. Give instruction to a wise man, and he will be yet wiser: teach a just man, and he will increase in learning."* Proverbs 9:8-9
>
> *The fear of the LORD (YHWH) is the beginning of wisdom: and the knowledge of the holy is understanding."* Proverbs 9:10
>
> *"A righteous man hateth lying: but a wicked man is loathsome, and cometh to shame."* Proverbs 13:5
>
> *"He that walketh with wise men shall be wise: but a companion of fools shall be destroyed."* Proverbs 13:20
>
> *"There is a way which seemeth right unto a man, but the end thereof are the ways of death."* Proverbs 14:12

> *The fear of the LORD (YHWH) is the beginning of wisdom: a good understanding have all they that do his commandments: his praise endureth forever."* Psalm 111:10
>
> *"Thou through thy commandments hast made me wiser than mine enemies: for they are ever with me. I have more understanding than all my teachers: for thy testimonies are my meditation. I understand more than the ancients, because I keep thy precepts."* Psalm 119:98-100
>
> *"By humility and the fear of the LORD (YHWH) are riches, honor and life."* Proverbs 22:4
>
> *"A lying tongue hateth those that are afflicted by it; and a flattering mouth worketh ruin."* Proverbs 26:28
>
> *"He that trusteth in his riches shall fall, but the righteous shall flourish as a branch."* Proverbs 11:28
>
> *"The blessing of the LORD (YHWH), it maketh rich, and he addeth no sorrow with it."* Proverbs 10:22

There are many other verses of profound wisdom and insight in these two books, but this list provides an ample list for us to work with. What are some of the key principles we can glean from these verses that distinguish the wise from the foolish and the righteous or upright from the wicked? Here are a few of the most important ones:

1. The prerequisites to knowledge, wisdom and understanding are to fear God and keep His commandments. So those who fail to fear God are both wicked and foolish. Unless one has a healthy reverence for and fear of the power of God to send any of us to hell any time He chooses, we lack the motivation and the ability to keep His commandments. God only reveals truth to those who fear Him and keep His commandments. Everyone else who does not do these things, He leaves in the dark and clueless.

2. Pride, flattery and lies are the telltale marks of a wicked fool. Humility, bringing kind correction (rebuke) to others out of genuine care for their welfare and

speaking the truth are the marks of a man of wisdom, righteousness, honor and virtue.

3. Bad company corrupts good character. If you hang out with people of seedy characters, your character will reflect their bad influences and you will become like them. Wise and godly men have nothing to do with those who manifest the traits of the wicked and the foolish.

4. Mockers, scorners and those who bear false witness against others are wicked fools and ought to be avoided and shunned.

5. Time and again, God reveals His hatred for lying and liars. God calls upon His people to be honest and of genuine integrity and trustworthiness and He reveals that He is the source of all truth. Conversely, the devil, God's created spirit being, is the father of lies and the destroyer. Each and every one of us is either of the truth or of the lie and what we manifest in our words and actions throughout our lives reveal who we really belong to: either God or the devil. There is no middle ground. We all are of one or the other.

6. Riches profit a man nothing if he gains the whole world, but loses his soul in the end and spends eternity in torment in the burning lake of fire and brimstone, as Revelation 21:8 teaches will be the end of all wicked liars and fools.

The underlying and unstated premise that all Trump and Q Anon supporters make is that both entities arc fundamentally truthful, trustworthy and of good character. If that's true, then both Trump and Q Anon's words and actions ought to corroborate and support that unstated, but underlying premise. Because their words and actions do not support that contention, then any claim that Trump is draining the swamp of the deep state is not the least bit credible either. As we shall see together, this is precisely the situation in which we find ourselves if we examine the hard facts and evidence with honesty and intellectual integrity and set our emotions and wishful thinking aside, as we properly should. Emotions and wishful thinking are, after all, no basis on which to base our conclusions that affect how we invest our lives and our attention in the remaining time we all have available to us to live wisely and prosperously.

Let's examine each of the six principles of wisdom and upright character I have summarized above with what is publicly known and available concerning Trump and Q Anon:

1. Does Donald Trump know and fear God and keep His commandments? During Trump's 2016 Presidential campaign, he was interviewed by Family Resource Council's President, Tony Perkins, who asked Trump if he had ever sought God's forgiveness. Trump avoided the issue, Perkins pressed him to address the question and Trump replied that he never had and simply does not think in those terms. Instead, he tries to do better the next time, he told his television audience. So, to put it succinctly, Donald Trump neither knows God nor does he fear Him. Because if he did, he would be on his knees seeking God's forgiveness for his serial adulteries that are public knowledge, among other sins that he has committed.

   A man who neither fears God, nor keeps His commandments, is seriously lacking in wisdom, honesty and integrity. Just because over 99% of all Americans are in this same boat does not and should not change our conclusion about Donald Trump and his character one iota.

2. Does Trump manifest a spirit of pride or humility? Does he engage in flattery and lies, or honesty and integrity? Trump clearly manifests a spirit of overweening pride and shamelessly engages in flattery of many people whose conduct is publicly known not to warrant praise, but rather disdain. In other words, Donald Trump tells many people what he thinks they want to hear about themselves, even if it is a bald-faced

and overt lie. His garish interior decorating tastes mirror the extensive use of gold and other symbols of extreme wealth in his Trump Tower suite and reveal a man who has no self-restraint and who suffers from over-weening pride and narcissism.

3. How about the company whom Donald Trump has kept most of his life? Are his companions men of honesty, competence and impeccable integrity? Or are they something materially short of this standard? Trump's companions and associates have included the likes of sodomite Jewish lawyer Roy Cohn, convicted pedophile Jeffrey Epstein, and organized crime bosses Hillary and Bill Clinton, whom Trump has described as his good friends in public television interviews. Trump has continued to surround himself with very seedy characters within his administration, many of whom are long-time Zionist warmongers and members of the CFR, or Council on Foreign Relations, the most publicly visible arm of the Illuminati in America since its founding in 1921 by Rothschild agent, Woodrow Wilson handler and White House Chief of Staff, Col. Edward Mandel House. Among these were former Secretary of State Mike Pompeo and war hawk John Bolton, both of whom were hell-bent on orchestrating false flag events in the Persian Gulf and promulgating endless lies of Iranian terrorist acts to try to start a war with Iran on behalf of America's Zionist puppet masters, Israel and Saudi Arabia. A careful examination of almost all of Trump's cabinet members would reveal that most of them were members of the CFR and long-standing members of the global elite conspiracy and these were the men and women who ran America into the ground quite intentionally. For example, former Treasury Secretary Steven Mnuchin is an Ashkenazi Jewish Wall Street bankster from Goldman Sachs, and former Commerce Secretary Wilbur Ross is an Ashkenazi Jew and the former Rothschild agent who was responsible for bailing Trump out of bankruptcy in 1992. If you don't

think there could be any connection between that financial transaction and Trump's selection as President in 2016, think again. Now you have a good idea of where Trump's true loyalties are likely to lie, and it's not with the American people, any more than than it was for any of his predecessors over the past three decades. Once again, we've all been had and conned.

4. Does Donald Trump avoid and shun mockers, scorners and those who bear false witness against others, including himself? This is one arena in which Trump performs admirably with the likes of Senate Minority Leader Chuck Schumer, House Speaker Nancy Pelosi, and Congressmen Adam Schiff and Jerrold Nadler, to name a few of his most deviant and dishonest political opponents. But having said this, it appears quite likely that all the Trump bashing that Washington D.C. and the MSM engaged in during the last four years was all contrived theater and diversionary tactics that Trump was fully in on and went along with.

5. Does Donald Trump ever lie? Does Q Anon? Yes, they both do. Trump has contradicted himself on gun control, asserting in connection with the high school false flag shooting incident in Parkland, Florida, that guns should be confiscated first and ask questions later (referring to red flag laws), after claiming when he ran for President that he was a staunch defender of Second Amendment rights for Americans to bear arms to defend themselves against government tyranny. Similarly, during the 2016 Presidential campaign and debates, Trump claimed that if he were elected, he would see to it that his opponent, Hillary Clinton, was investigated for her past actions. Yet shortly after he was elected, Trump gave a television interview in which he stated that Hillary and Bill Clinton were good

people and that he would not have the Clintons investigated for their potentially illegal acts.

Likewise, in Q Post #2622 on December 12, 2018, a Q follower posed the following question: "Just to shut the Flat Earthers up Q, Is the Earth flat?" Q replied, "No." I have already proven the flat earth to be the objective truth in my first book, *Making Sense Out of a World Gone* Mad, at pages 226-230.

Anyone foolish enough to engage in lying fails to understand that when caught in one's lies, the wise will never give a proven liar any credibility or trust ever again. This is not to suggest that Trump's apparent political opponents and the media do not lie profusely, because they both do. But when everyone is lying, a wise man will trust no one and walk away in disgust, which is what we all ought to be doing in response to the charade and theater of fraudulent and corrupt American politics ruled by demon-possessed psychopaths and pathological liars, all of whom serve the devil, the father of lies and the destroyer. Nothing could be any more obvious than this.

Many of those who identify themselves as Trump fans and Q Anon supporters routinely claim that the truth is the first casualty in any war and that deception, lies, and disinformation are standard tools of informational, psychological and conventional warfare. While all of this may be true, anyone who makes his living as a professional liar is a tool of the devil, the father of lies and the destroyer. There are no exceptions to this. As a nation and as a culture, the vast majority of Americans have no clue and no interest in what the truth is any longer and so they have no solid foundation on which to decide whom, if anyone, to trust and follow. Those who pose as leaders who ever lie to their followers, have no business leading anything and are unfit to be true leaders worthy of anyone following them and are a risk to themselves. Sadly, this is where we find ourselves today. It reduces the few of us who remain sane and of the truth to recognize that the only sensible way to live in a world of insanity and madness is to place all our trust in YHWH (God) alone, the God of truth, because without Him, we are all screwed and headed to our own destruction.

6. Donald Trump boasted during the 2016 Presidential campaign of a personal net worth of some $7 billion. Yahushua tells us in Matthew 19:23-24,

   > *"Verily I say unto you, That a rich man shall hardly enter into the kingdom of heaven, And again I say unto you, It is easier for a camel to go through the eye of needle, than for a rich man to enter into the kingdom of God."*

   Those who are rich in this life almost always make their wealth and affluence their god and idol and thus will compromise everything, including their souls, their integrity and their honor, to hold onto their illusion of being in control of their destiny. The simple truth is that none of us are. Only God is and He is on the brink of proving it to all of us conclusively and quite dramatically very soon. When it happens, no amount of wealth will save the ungodly sinner from perishing for all eternity. This clearly is Donald Trump's eternal fate, predestinated for him by God. Those who cannot yet see this are themselves bound for the same eternal damnation by a just, holy and righteous God, YHWH, who has just about had enough of mankind's wickedness and folly.

Other Compromising Facts

I revealed earlier that every politician not only lies well, but has one or more embarrassing indiscretions in their pasts, which their globalist puppet masters know all about, which makes them easily compromised and blackmailed. So what have been Donald Trump's compromising indiscretions? It's a matter of broad public knowledge that he has committed adultery with multiple women, which today's culture brushes off as no big deal, even though it reflects very badly on the man's character and loyalty to his wife and family.

What is quite a bit more troubling is that Wayne Madsen, in his Wayne Madsen Report, reports six instances he has uncovered in which Donald Trump paid fairly large legal settlements totaling roughly $40 million to six minors (3 females and 3 males), ages 10 to 13, whom Madsen alleges Trump raped from 1989 to 2012. [25] If these allegations concerning Donald Trump are true, which they quite likely are, we can be quite certain that Trump was fully compromised and easily blackmailed by his globalist puppet masters. Moreover, sex with children (pedophilia) almost always, if not universally, results in those who engage in such heinous acts becoming demon-possessed and owned by the devil. In fact, it's why most of them do it. Sadly, this appears to be how the game of hardball, high stakes politics in America is played by all those who wield substantial political power and influence in this country, and Trump appears to be no exception.

Furthermore, Trump's niece, Mary L. Trump, who holds a PhD in clinical psychology, published an embarrassing book in 2020 entitled, *Too Much and Never Enough: How my Family Created the World's Most Dangerous Man,* about her uncle in which she reveals that Trump had actively schemed to try to trick his aging father to sign a codicil to his will that would have had the effect of leaving his entire estate to his son, Donald, and would have effectively disinherited his four siblings and their offspring. While ultimately, Trump's father Fred, did not go

---

[25] *Why is Trump so afraid of Cohen's testimony?* https://www.waynemadsenreport.com. January 14-15, 2019.

along with his son's cunning attempts to defraud his siblings and their families, the fact that Trump would even consider engaging in such treachery and betrayal of his own family members reveals precisely why he could be equally expected to betray America and the American people, if it suited him.

5. What We Should Have Expected to Happen if Trump was Truly Going to Drain the Swamp

Many American patriots who view themselves as Trump and Q Anon supporters recognize that America is a nation in dire straits, ruled by many deviant liars who these Trump and Q Anon supporters identify as Communists, liberals and Democrats. This is a big mistake. The depth and nature of what ails America and the rest of the world at their core is of a profoundly spiritual nature. How this spiritual war manifests itself in the political realm confuses and deceives almost everyone and this is by YHWH's (God's) predestinated design. Even if I explain here what is really happening in spiritual terms, most people will still not get it. They will simply dismiss it, because God has chosen not to reveal these sorts of things to them. From my vantage point, this is profoundly frustrating. I long for everyone to be able to see and understand what I am blessed by YHWH to be able to see and understand. But I cannot, and I fully understand and accept that this is part of God's sovereign will, to which I must, and I have chosen to, submit.

We are facing a world that is not at all what it appears to be on the surface. There is an elephant in the room and we all are like blind men groping different parts of the elephant and arriving at distinctly different conclusions as to the nature of the beast we have our hold on, and unless God chooses to reveal the conundrum to all of us, we will be forever at odds with one another.

If we all see the battlefield and the enemy differently, we will all conclude that our own unique understanding is the objective truth and everyone else is confused, if not quite insane. The key to resolving this is to put 100% of our trust in God, fear Him, keep His commandments and submit our lives and our wills fully to Him. He alone sees all things clearly. None of the rest of us can be completely confident that we do, and this is precisely as He has intended it all along. It's a bit frustrating, isn't it? At least I find it so.

Having said this, in Chapters 3 and 4 I have painted a rather stark and different view of the elephant in the room than most people dare to consider or examine. If my stark picture of objective, universal and absolute reality is accurate, then what would it take to reverse a process that has been under way for centuries that God has intentionally planned and allowed to bring us to this point of time in world history? Answering this question is the purpose of this chapter. In doing so, I will be revealing why no plan to reverse what has been directed by God for centuries can ever be implemented effectively. Simply put, God has no intention of allowing such a plan to ever be put into action, because that does not serve His sovereign purpose and will. This is because God has no intention of sharing His glory with anyone. And what God wills, He always gets.

What follows is a strategy and set of tactics that would be required to address the world as I have accurately described it in Chapter 3 of this book and reverse the damage done to date by the Luciferian global elite conspiracy that rules our world today.

If Donald Trump had been truly dedicated to draining the swamp of Washington D.C. effectively, he would have had to take the bold and radical approach of speaking the absolute truth all the time to the American people and doing that which is right in all his actions. If he failed to do this, his attempts to conceal his real motives and actions from portions of the country who he viewed as his adversaries, would undermine his ability to garner and retain the trust, credibility and support of the truly honest and righteous Americans who he ought to have been serving and draining the swamp for. In truth, we now know from Chapter 4 that Trump lacks the character, the will and the ability to do such a thing. But for sake of discussion, let's consider what it would take to rid ourselves of the demon-possessed psychos who rule our nation and world today.

If Donald Trump was devoted to doing whatever it took to save America from the evil that engulfs it, he would have done the following:

Day One

On Inauguration Day, January 20, 2017, Trump would have used the special forces of the U.S. military, whom he knew he could trust to execute his orders faithfully and fully, to round up, arrest and try before military tribunals a very large number of people in government, the media, corporate America, academia, Hollywood, Wall Street and many charitable organizations whose criminal, immoral and treasonous acts have undermined our nation and sought to overthrow our constitutional republic form of government and the rule of law.

Thanks to the revelations of former CIA and NSA contractor and whistleblower Edward Snowden, it is widely known that our government in the form of the NSA has been gathering, cataloging and saving every electronic and telephone communication we all have been making for at least the last 20 years. Consequently, properly directed by individuals with the technical expertise and moral integrity and devotion to duty, the information exists to fairly easily identify and charge high level government and other officials with treasonous and seriously criminal conduct and arrest and try them for such crimes before military tribunals, with swift and sure execution of their sentences to deliver real justice and restore credibility to our nation's institutions and the impartiality of the rule of law, applied equally to all persons.

These arrests would have had to occur in secrecy and great speed to neutralize the command and control structure of the global elite conspiracy with all due haste and comprehensive thoroughness. It has been widely reported that the U.S. Naval

Base at Guantanamo Bay, Cuba, known as GITMO, and an overflow base in central Honduras that is run by the U.S. military, have been materially expanded over the last four years, ostensibly in anticipation of conducting such military tribunals in secure locations. But perhaps that was just a ploy to mislead his supporters.

At the same time, he would need to have declared martial law and employed the armed services (again, whom he knew he could trust to execute his orders fully and faithfully) to shut down the CIA, DOJ, FBI, mainstream media (MSM), Big Tech social media (in the form of Facebook, YouTube, Twitter, Instagram and Google), the entirety of the U.S. Congress and the federal judiciary. Trump's first objective ought to have been to silence the main sources of opposition to his taking back control of the government from the global elite conspiracy by using overwhelming physical force and the element of surprise to catch his adversaries totally off guard and shut them down from effective counter attacks.

Sadly, our local, state and federal judiciaries are completely compromised, blackmailed and corrupt. Almost every judge and lawyer in America is a member of the secret society of Freemasonry, which from the top is ruled as a secret cult of Satan worship, as freely admitted in *Morals and Dogma,* by Albert Pike, Sovereign Grand Commander of the Scottish Rite of Freemasonry, in his 1871 book and bible of Freemasonry. Freemasonry would have to be banned and abolished and anyone who is or has been a past member in it, must never have been allowed to serve in any public office for the rest of his or her life. This is why civilian courts could not be relied upon to mete out justice that is so desperately needed in this nation, and that is the reason why military tribunals, following the military code of law against enemy combatants, and swiftly executing its sentences, would have been essential to use in place of civilian courts and the civilian code of law and legal practices.

The biggest problem with this hypothetical move is the trustworthiness of the U.S. military. Simply put, the U.S.

military is also extensively under the control of the secret society of Freemasonry and the Illuminati that controls Freemasonry in secret from within. From reports I have heard and read, most service men and women have been actively encouraged for decades to join Freemasonry as a way to gain promotions and advancement in the military. By the time a service person reaches flag rank officer (general or admiral) my understanding is that virtually everyone at that level are members of Freemasonry and loyal to the directions and orders of the lodges of Freemasonry, which is ruled by treachery and deceit from top to bottom. Thus, any President or leader who sought to employ martial law to overthrow our globalist puppet masters would almost certainly have been met by treachery and betrayals by members of the military loyal to Freemasonry.

The other major problem created by this hypothetical move would have been the likely response of somewhere between 20% and 50% of the U.S. populace who identify with the godless liberal side of American politics which is ruled by demon-spirit power. Such a move by Trump would almost certainly have resulted in riots in the streets and acts of violence and sabotage that would have had to be met with swift, sure and lethal military force. Could the U.S. military have been counted upon to deliver such lethal force, if called upon to do so by their Commander-in-Chief? In light of the former consideration of Freemasonry in the military, I highly doubt it.

The third problem with this first hypothetical move of Trump against the deep state would have been the likely response of the international community, all of whom are ruled by the same Luciferian global elite cabal. They are all members of the same cabal of Freemasonry and the Illuminati that quite likely Donald Trump is a member of too. If Trump had launched such an initiative on Day One, a contingent of international military forces from around the world would have likely threatened to invade the United States and overthrow the martial law that Trump might have ordered.

Fourth, international trade and domestic commerce would have been immediately and adversely impacted by Trump's declaration of martial law, no matter how clearly and effectively it was explained to the American people. With Americans' livelihoods adversely impacted, popular support for the imposition of martial law in America might have quickly vanished.

Day Two

Immediately after shutting down the mainstream media, Trump would have had to replace the absence of television, newspaper and Big Tech social media with a direct form of communication between himself and the American people on a daily basis to calm people's nerves and inform them, at least in a general sense, of moves being taken and the reasons for them. The most likely means for doing this would have been via the use of the Emergency Broadcast System to inform and educate a seriously deceived and often delusional American and international public.

Such an alternative media communications channel would, over time, have to have been replaced with an effective state-operated mass media operation which would have to have been distinguished by an exceptional level of honesty, integrity and candor with the American people. Virtually everything the American people today believe to be true is false, by intentional design of the CIA's Operation Mockingbird program, in which one former CIA Director, William Colby, once revealed,

> "We'll know our disinformation program is complete when everything the American public believes is false." [26]

In Chapter 8 of my book, *Making Sense Out of a World Gone Mad,* I reveal, expose and explain 24 of the most horrendous lies that have been taught to all of us over the last one hundred years, which has made intelligent and civil sharing of knowledge and important information almost impossible today. Simply put, this would have had to change and the results of opening the

---

[26] www.hcpress.com/letters-to-the-editor/letters-nwo=quotes.html

public's eyes to the objective reality of a nation and world gone mad would have inevitably produced, at least initially, severe cognitive dissonance, social distress, anger and confusion. But if the goal was to truly reverse the hijacking of our nation by the global elite cabal and its secret societies, there is nothing short of full transparency and disclosure that would have accomplished this and equipped the public with the education and knowledge so that they could never be hoodwinked and taken hostage by evil, demon-possessed psychopaths ever again.

Sadly, our nation's founding fathers fully realized that the day would eventually arrive in which America would succumb to insidious forces which would inevitably infiltrate, corrupt and hijack our once moral and God-fearing nation from within. This is precisely what has happened today, spear-headed by the God-hating Talmudic Jews who rule over the global elite conspiracy of Satan worshippers and secret societies that John F. Kennedy warned us about in 1961. On October 11, 1798, President John Adams, stated in his address to the military:

> *"We have no government armed with power capable of contending with human passions unbridled by morality and religion. Avarice, ambition, revenge or gallantry, would break the strongest cords of our Constitution as a whale goes through a net. Our Constitution was made only for a moral and religious people. It is wholly inadequate to the government of any other."* [27]

Sadly, in 2021, America is not the least bit a moral, religious, educated, wise, or knowledgeable people any longer.

<u>Day Three</u>

As of this writing, the officially acknowledged national debt of the United States stands at $27.8 trillion. In addition, Michigan State University Professor Dr. Mark Skidmore, aided by a team of graduate students of his in accounting, uncovered an additional $21 trillion of funds that have not been accounted

---

[27] Federer, William J. *America's God and Country Encyclopedia of Quotations.* pp. 10-11.

for in the financial statements and operations of the Department of Defense (DOD) and Department of Housing and Urban Development (HUD) prior to 2016. This latter amount was classified according to FASAB Rule #56 as a matter of national security that cannot be publicly discussed. So your government has used obfuscation and deception to cover up a massive financial crime and act of fraud. The upshot of all of this is that America's national debt today hovers around $48 trillion and is growing rapidly and by design to bankrupt this nation and make the U.S. Dollar worthless. This is not some esoteric accounting matter that very few people know about. Quite the contrary is the truth; most financial experts and economists are well aware of the grave circumstances facing our nation and currency and the honest and forthright ones freely admit that America is facing a financial calamity of unfathomable proportions and virtually no one is offering any credible options for solving this looming crisis.

The looming debt crisis and likely collapse of the value of the U.S. Dollar has been deliberately engineered this way by the synagogue of Satan's agents of the disingenuously named Federal Reserve Bank. In reality, the global elite cabal orchestrated the passage of the Federal Reserve Act of 1913, which they themselves wrote and secretly promoted, that grants an exclusive monopoly to a private bank, owned and controlled by the global elite cabal, to print money out of thin air and loan it to the United States corporation, backed by the income taxing authority of the Internal Revenue Service, pursuant to a fraudulently ratified Sixteenth Amendment to the United States Constitution in February 1913. [28]

During the George W. Bush, Obama and Trump Presidencies, the nation's annual federal deficit has ballooned to over $1 trillion a year and the interest and principal repayments have

---

[28] Benson, Bill and Beckman, M.J. 'Red.' *The Law That Never Was - The fraud of the 16th Amendment and personal Income Tax.* 1985.

been rolled over into new debt instruments with no hope of the national debt ever being paid down, much less paid off. This financial skullduggery and sleight of hand is euphemistically referred to as "quantitative easing." Normally such practices would be highly inflationary, but in the last 20 years, America's real economy has been in a sustained recession, if not depression, were it not for the inflationary effects of this excessive money printing and debt financing, which only delays and exacerbates the eventual collapse of the U.S. Dollar as the world's primary reserve currency. The only reason that America as a nation has gotten away with its reckless and irresponsible financial mismanagement and fraud has been that the military budget of the United States is equal that of the next eight largest military budgets in the world and our military has been used to threaten and extort other nations into continuing to go along with this most monstrous Ponzi scheme in all of world history.

The only other option over and above continuing to print money is for the UNITED STATES corporation to default on its debt and declare bankruptcy, thereby renegotiating the terms of the debt and its repayment. Normally, such a bankruptcy would result in the creditors who own the debt, acquiring a controlling interest in the bankrupt corporation. Those who hold the majority of the nation's debt instruments are other nations and the richest families in the world, who not coincidentally also sit at the top of the global elite conspiracy cabal and who have aims to merge all the nations of the world together under a one world government structure that they secretly own and control, in which the rest of the world's sharply reduced population (through war, famines and pestilences) would become their obedient slaves.

On December 21, 2017, President Trump issued Executive Order #13818, Blocking the Property of Persons Involved in Serious Human Rights Abuse or Corruption, which authorizes the seizing of the assets of persons or entities found guilty of serious human rights abuses or corruption. Since the wealthiest people in the world, who hold the vast majority of America's national debt, have engaged in human sex trafficking, Satanic

Ritual Abuse (SRA), and drug and gun running and have engaged in overt corruption and fraud to impoverish the American people under false pretexts and pretenses, a shrewd warrior and general would recognize that resolving America's national debt crisis is not a financial or legal issue, but rather an issue of who has the greatest physical force and the will to use it to get his way with his adversaries (in this case, America's creditors).

Up to now, the heads of the Jewish global elite banking families have used the threat of war and the threat of extortion to force the world's leaders to continue to honor their countries' national debt obligations. But if Trump had been committed to breaking the back of the global elite conspiracy and deep state, he would have had to be prepared to use the overwhelming force and might of the American military to covertly round up and arrest a number of the globalist kingpins and seize their substantial assets, which would include the majority of the national debt of the UNITED STATES corporation. It is virtually certain that other members of these globalist families would respond to such a provocative move, were Trump to have made it, by inducing one or more other countries to attack the United States in the hope that the United States' military could be defeated and/or undermined from within. China, North Korea and Iran would have been the most likely candidates to launch a military attack against the United States. But given the vast disparity in military spending between the United States and the eight nations with the next largest military budgets, threatening the United States with a military attack would have been fraught with risk for the globalists.

The other ace that the Jewish globalists have had up their sleeves is the threat of extortion. Here is how these devil worshipping Jews have so delicately put it in their own writings and teachings:

> "You may say that the goyim will rise upon us, arms in hand, if they guess what is going on before the time comes; but in the West we have against this a manoeuvre

> of such appalling terror that the very stoutest hearts quail - the undergrounds, metropolitans, those subterranean corridors which, before the time comes, will be driven under all the capitals and from whence those capitals will be blown into the air with all their organizations and archives." [29]

In January, 2021, we witnessed 30,000 National Guard troops stationed in Washington DC on the eve of the inauguration of Joe Biden as President in a monstrously fraudulent election and FEMA appeared to have been activated and in control of our nation's capital to help the residents of that city cope with the aftermath of what appeared to have been some horrific planned violence or false flag attack. Could it have been that Trump and his advisors anticipated the detonation of an explosive nuclear device hidden somewhere within the subways of that city for a time such as this? Nothing is out of the question at this point. So the question for Trump became, how much would he have been willing to risk the potential deaths of tens of thousands of civilians and soldiers to stare down his adversaries who have the entire world by the balls as its creditors? And what would have motivated his military commanders to comply with his orders when virtually all flag rank officers are likely members of Freemasonry, which is secretly controlled from the top by the leading devil-worshipping Talmudic Jews of the global elite conspiracy?

If Trump were to have pulled this off some way, if the military had been able to locate and confiscate the vast preponderance of assets of the global elite conspirators and disavow honoring the debt held by these murderous criminals, he could have ordered the U.S. Treasury to print new U.S. Dollars (not federal reserve notes) backed by a reinstituted gold standard, to pay for the expenses of operating the federal government, assuming that the United States had or confiscated a large enough tonnage of gold to be able back these new and distinguishable U.S. Treasury Dollars. Having said that, those

---

[29] *Protocols of the Meetings of the Learned Elders of Zion.* Protocol No. 9, last paragraph. p. 27.

holding assets denominated in Federal Reserve note dollars would have inevitably sustained large losses on such assets unless Trump and his team could have conceived of a way to keep the little guy whole, while dishonoring any such assets held by global elite criminals.

Day Four

The United States government has allowed dual citizenship and dual allegiances to exist in America and many such individuals serve with divided loyalties in their capacities as government officials. This should have never been tolerated or permitted. Nowhere is this practice more insidiously tolerated than it is with those holding dual Israeli/U.S. citizenship and it would have needed to be stopped immediately. Dual citizenship and dual loyalties ought to have been declared null and void and all those holding such dual citizenship ought to have been barred from holding any position in any form of government in the United States and those in such positions at the time of this order ought to have been terminated immediately. The presumption always should have been that a dual loyalty or citizenship is tantamount to disloyalty, if not an enemy combatant, to the United States.

In addition to dual Israeli/U.S. citizenship, Catholics, Jews, Freemasons, members of the Council on Foreign Relations and any other secret societies a person belongs to should have disqualified them from serving in any government capacity in America.

Under President Jimmy Carter, legislation was passed authorizing the creation of a Senior Executive Service, the SES, which accounts for roughly 5,000 of the most senior policy-making positions in our federal government from which SES members cannot be fired. Since the Carter administration, these career government executives have run the federal bureaucracy and made it increasingly difficult for any President to alter America's domestic or foreign policies. This situation too is intolerable and should have been ended immediately.

To make matters even more complicated, my understanding is that almost every cabinet level department in the United States federal "system" is a separate legal corporation with its own independent board of directors that does not answer to the President of the UNITED STATES corporation. And who are the members of the board of directors that the President reports to? Almost no one has any idea what the answer to this very important question is. Either way, we can be certain that no President is accountable to the American voters, even though we have been told all our lives that they are, or should be. It's all just one more in a set of monstrous lies. To deal with this intolerable situation effectively, the legal facts would have had to have been rooted out and every corporate institution posing as a government entity should have been legally dissolved. Many of them should never have been reconstituted as branches of the government since their missions and mandates have vastly exceeded the responsibilities of the federal government laid out for all of us in the United States Constitution and should have been abolished. But of course, every such entity has a favored special interest group whose interests these corporate entities have served, so the hue and cry associated with the closure of each such pseudo-government institution would have been almost unimaginable and quite daunting to deal with.

Day 5

Trump ought to have issued an Executive Order announcing the closure of all federal bureaucracies not in furtherance of the U.S. Constitution, naming every institution that fell under this designation. Such an Executive Order ought to have called for an aggressive plan to rescind and simplify as many federal laws and regulations as possible. The goal of the federal government (not corporation) ought to be to protect the safety of American citizens; not to give unfair advantages and special privileges to favored special interests. Again, any attempt to implement such measures would inevitably be met with a hue and cry by these same special interest groups which have derived unfair advantages at the expense of their fellow Americans for years, if not decades.

5. What We Should Have Expected to Happen if Trump was Truly Going to Drain the Swamp

Day 6

Trump would need to have issued an Executive Order making it a felony for any government official to lie or knowingly make false statements to the public. Today we have the opposite situation and nothing any government official or the media with whom they are in cahoots is the least bit honest, and it's perfectly legal to lie to the American people, whom they allegedly serve (but in reality, do not). We all know this and tolerate what amounts to an intolerable situation. It would have needed to stop. Those entrusted with directing the public affairs of this country ought to have been beyond reproach. Instead, we have the most treacherous liars and thieves brazenly stuffing their wallets and the wallets of their family members at the public trough and getting away with lying about all of it with complete impunity.

Day 7

Americans have been subjected to numerous programs and operations to harm our health and diminish our mental acuity so that we, as a populace, are brainwashed, clueless and docile. It would have required a massive and coordinated education campaign of the public as to the dangers of many harmful technologies and substances to which we have been subjected, combined with an aggressive campaign to shut down a number of these operations, to halt this assault on our awareness of what has been going on for decades behind our backs.

First on the list must have been television technology, which was originally designed to be a hypnotic mind control programming technology to implant subliminal messaging in the minds of its viewers without them being aware of it. The media strategy would have needed to educate the public about the dangers of television and urge that the public discard their televisions or sharply curtail their use.

The chemtrail program, that is international in scope, would have needed to be shut down immediately. For at least 20 years, military aircraft equipped with chemical tanks, plumbing and nozzles have been spraying toxic chemicals including aluminum, barium, strontium and biological agents such as Morgellons into our ionosphere in pursuit of multiple nefarious objectives, including weather modification and weather warfare, capturing the frequencies of target civilian population brain waves for psychological mind control, and remote application of Directed Energy Weapon (DEW) technology to ignite false flag event wildfires to terrorize civilian populations and to drive them from their homes. The spraying programs conducted by the secret military and civilian aircraft worldwide would have needed to be shut down immediately and the public educated about the existence and multiple uses of this technology and its various health dangers, including an increased incidence of Alzheimer's Disease and Autism caused by elevated levels of aluminum in our air, water, soil and food.

Similarly, all scheduled and mandatory vaccinations ought to have been shut down immediately. The 1986 federal act granting immunity to vaccine manufacturers ought to have been immediately repealed and the public would have needed to be educated on the very real dangers and extent of adverse health reactions to this highly questionable health technology of vaccines derived from animal diseases. The DVD, *VAXXED,* documents the horrific tale of the extent to which the Center for Disease Control concealed compelling evidence of a link between the administration of the Measles, Mumps and Rubella (MMR) vaccine and a materially increased incidence of diagnoses of Autism following MMR vaccination for a large number of children. Autism has increased from a diagnosis of 1 out of every 10,000 children some 50 years ago, to at least 1 out of every 50 children today, that is highly correlated with a very alarming increase in the recommended and enforced vaccination schedule for American children. It amounts to a deliberate program to harm the health of America's children and health and it would have needed to stop immediately and permanently.

Substances such as fluoride are being added to many communities' water supplies, ostensibly to reduce the incidence of dental decay, but fluoride has the effect of reducing the mental acuity of those consuming fluoridated water over significant periods of time. This practice ought to have been banned and made illegal for this reason.

For roughly 100 years, the dental industry, spurred on by the American Dental Association's ownership of the patents on it, has been filling the cavities of American dental patients with silver-amalgam fillings consisting of 50% mercury, a known carcinogen, which then leaches into the dental patient's body for the rest of his or her life or until those fillings are removed and replaced with bio-compatible dental filling materials. [30] This practice would have needed to be fully exposed and made unlawful to prevent its continuance.

Similarly, Genetically Modified Organism (GMO) foods have been introduced into our food supply over the last 20 years without any credible studies of the long-term effects upon consumers' health. Until such studies have been conducted by independent researchers without a conflict of interest which conclusively establish the safety of such GMO foods, they ought to have been banned for sale.

Collectively, these programs have been deliberately designed by the Satan-worshipping global elites to exterminate a large portion of the world's human population, while preserving the excuse of "plausible deniability" for its scientific community perpetrators. As such, these programs amount to crimes against humanity for which the corporations and scientists involved in perpetrating these criminal and immoral acts would have needed to be tried in accordance with the international laws against crimes against humanity, and punished accordingly.

<u>Day 8</u>

Trump would have had to address head-on the secret loyalty oaths taken by various groups of people serving in public office which, from proven experience, have manifested a willingness

---

[30] Huggins, Dr. Hal. *Client Education Packet.* Huggins Applied Healing, Colorado Springs, CO, 2012. pp. 51-52.

to engage in secret societies and conspiracies to engage in criminal and immoral acts to the harm of their fellow citizens. These include but are not limited to Jews, Catholics, lawyers and Freemasons. The practices of the Jews throughout the last 2,600 years reveal that they are an immoral and seditious religious cult and culture who have used lies and cunning to gain an unfair advantage over their fellow citizens and to demonize anyone who has the audacity to call them on it. *The Protocols of the Learned Elders of Zion*, from which I have quoted previously in this book, reveals a plan of global domination of almost unthinkable evils from which there can be no denials. Membership in the Jewish community and having been raised in a Jewish family virtually guarantees demon-possession in everyone involved in that community and ought to have resulted in an Executive Order expelling all Jews, Catholics, lawyers and Freemasons from public service for life and making it a felony to conceal one's identity in these organizations and communities from one's employer.

Catholics are effectively dual citizens of the Vatican city-state and the United States. Their loyalties are divided between the Roman Catholic Church as an institution, as embodied in the Catholic Pope, to whom absolute obedience is demanded by this religious cult, versus the United States and the rest of us.

Freemasons swear oaths that swear allegiance to the lodge of Freemasonry and their leaders that supersede and trump any federal, state or local government oaths of office that a Freemason may swear or take. Given the nefarious history of Freemasonry, anyone swearing an oath to conceal and never reveal the secrets of the lodge of Freemasonry to any outsiders is unqualified and unfit for public service and office.

Similarly, all lawyers are members of the BAR association, a British barrister's trade association from which all lawyers derive their rights to practice law in the United States. Lawyers as a profession are widely known to be treacherous, money-grubbing liars. The legal profession attracts and appeals to the most unsavory of characters who almost always manifest no moral scruples that also makes them unfit for public office. Serving in public office is not a right but a privilege and an honor, and office holders ought to have been held accountable for remaining that way by enforcing codes of honest and moral conduct beyond reproach. The groups of people singled out here have a long history of conduct that makes them woefully unqualified for honest public service.

Day 9

Because the Sixteenth Amendment authorizing the income tax was not legally ratified by a single one of the 38 states that allegedly ratified it in 1913, and because Trump should have declared the national debt null and void on Day 2 of his Presidency in 2017, he should have also issued another Executive Order declaring the Sixteenth Amendment rescinded because of the fraudulent way it was ratified, as amply documented in Bill Benson's and M.J. 'Red' Beckman's 1985 book, *The Law That Never Was*, and abolish the Internal Revenue Service and the income tax, thereby returning more of the people's rightful income back to them, as Trump aggressively cut back the scope of the federal government to its constitutionally permitted mandates and to reduce federal spending.

In addition, in order to send a clear signal to the American citizens, Trump ought to have issued another Executive Order, related to this one, that rescinds the 1954 Johnson Act which created the abomination of the 501(c)3 tax exempt churches that have been concealing the truth of the global conspiracy and its many workings from their congregations in order to maximize their tax exemption benefits, to the very real harm of their congregations. I fully document the restrictions imposed by the IRS on 501(c)3 churches in Chapter 11 of my first book, *Making Sense Out of a World Gone Mad*. It has had the effect of turning American churches into apostate, empty shells of the spiritually dead and it is despicable what pastors and boards of elders have allowed to be done in their churches in pursuit of mammon (i.e. the almighty dollar).

Day 10

The election and voter fraud of November 3, 2020 laid out a large number of the ploys used by deep state liars and frauds to manipulate vote counts and reports of the results. It's not the least bit rocket science; elections are deliberately rigged all the time. This is why incumbents seldom lose their bids for re-election. Thus, Trump would have had to hire an outside consulting firm to diagnose the root causes of voter and election fraud and recommend a strategy for eliminating those root causes so that voters could be assured that votes cast by voters would be accurately counted and reported and that no voters ineligible to vote would be permitted to have their votes counted, along with an aggressive timeline for executing their proposed plan nationwide.

Even more significantly, it is important to recognize that voters are always presented with two moral deviants as political candidates to choose between (such as between Donald Trump and Joe Biden). So regardless of who you vote for, it really doesn't matter, because both choices are profound losers and charlatans. And besides, over 95% of the population are naive and unsophisticated fools who know nothing about what wise and effective leadership looks like. Thus, choosing our leaders by allowing stupid people to express their naive and emotional feelings to select their leaders could not be more foolish or fruitless.

Day 11

Obamacare is a disaster. This is because the government is inserting itself into our health care decisions and making our healthcare industry controlled by government bureaucrats who have an agenda to keep us sick. The key would have been if Trump got the government out of regulating healthcare in every respect. Forget health insurance except catastrophic health care insurance in the event you contract a financially devastating health condition. Trump should have issued an Executive Order that required all healthcare providers to publish public price lists of treatments and services offered, in which a government-funded outside agency or company compiles and reports the results of customer (patient) reviews that are focused on measuring the results achieved from treatments provided by different healthcare providers. Allow results to speak for themselves: both results and their costs (prices). Transform the patient into a paying customer and health and wellness costs would go down. No longer support government programs which favor allopathic medicine over holistic medicine. Let the results and the costs speak for themselves.

Day 12

Trump would have needed to emasculate and defang the deep state organized crime syndicate by declassifying and releasing for publication to the internet the truth concerning the following events:

1. The JFK assassination orchestrated by the CIA, the Israeli Mossad and Meyer Lansky's Jewish Mafia and how it was executed
2. The 1967 attack by Israel on the USS Liberty and its subsequent cover up
3. The inside job and false flag attack of 9/11: how it was executed and what its true objectives were
4. The Oklahoma City bombing
5. The alleged suicide of Jeffrey Epstein

Day 13

Launch comprehensive public education programs via the internet teaching the truth concerning:

1. Evidence for a flat earth
2. Evidence for creationism v. Darwinism
3. Realities of space travel and man's alleged moon landings and how they were faked
4. Evidence (or lack thereof) of man-made global warming and the real agenda of the liars behind this fraud

5. The holohoax
6. True teachings of the Babylonian Talmud and Zohar Kabbalah of orthodox Judaism
7. History of the fake Jews (synagogue of Satan) since the Babylonian exile
8. Contents of the *Protocols of the Learned Elders of Zion*
9. Known causes of cancer and natural cures for it
10. Documented facts and study results of vaccine effectiveness and safety
11. Sex trafficking and drug and gun running operations of the U.S. government (CIA and others) and the global elite

The bottom line is that at a minimum, these steps would need to have been taken to decisively expose and demolish the control systems of the global elite conspiracy or deep state. Any clearly thinking reader and student of our world should be able to see that the powerful and entrenched special interest groups which would be exposed and neutered by these actions would have done whatever it took, including murder, bribes, extortion and the perpetration of an endless string of false flag events to terrorize the American people and our nominal leaders and puppets into submission to put a conclusive halt to these measures, so as to preserve their hard fought unfair advantages that they enjoy today at the expense of the rest of us.

Simply put, this is why Trump could not have ever drained the swamp and why no man or group of men, no matter how brilliant and cunning they might be, could ever defeat this monstrous behemoth of pure evil in the service of the devil, the father of lies and the destroyer. He's not known as that in the Bible for nothing. This is also why only an all-powerful God can step in to crush this demonic rebellion conclusively, once and for all. It is no coincidence that this is precisely what the Bible tells us in Revelation 19 and 20 is what will soon happen in order to rid God's creation of evil once and for all, forever.

6. Clues that Trump is a Card-Carrying Swamp Rat Just Like all the Rest

Now that we have examined and thought through together what it would require of anyone to defeat the global elite conspiracy, we should have concluded that it is virtually impossible for any man or group of men to do such a thing, because the globalist beast political and economic system has infiltrated, corrupted and hijacked virtually every institution and every position of leadership the world over. This was the very position that history Professor Caroll Quigley articulated in his 1966 book, *Tragedy and Hope,* in which he hoped to persuade all his readers to abandon any hope of reversing what had been a centuries-old progression toward the New World Order global surveillance and police state from hell, as depicted in Fabian Socialist George Orwell's deliberately prophetic novel, *1984*. Today, in 2021, we are there. However, to put the final nails in the coffin of this murder mystery, it is also instructive to examine some of the actions which Donald Trump took during his four years in office as America's most recent in a long line of puppets, actors and stooges.

One of the first clues that Trump was not at all who he pretended to be were those who financially backed him in his run for the Presidency in 2016. Zionist Jew and Las Vegas casino operator Sheldon Adelson topped the list of Trump's financial backers, but the line of wealthy and powerful New York Ashkenazi Jews who backed Trump in his 2016 campaign and who financed his inauguration in January of 2017 reads like a Who's Who of the Jewish elites. Trump went on to stack his cabinet with Ashkenazi Jews such as Treasury Secretary and former Goldman Sachs partner, Steve Mnuchin, and Commerce Secretary and former Rothschild banking agent, Wilbur Ross, who was instrumental in bailing Trump out of bankruptcy in 1992, and Trump's administration was no less packed with members of the Council on Foreign Relations (CFR) than were the administrations of his more recent predecessors. This fact alone shouts volumes that Trump was merely the latest in a long string of puppets and stooges owned and controlled by the Ashkenazi Jews and the CFR, who always do their bidding.

Shortly after taking office, Trump ordered that the U.S. Embassy in Tel Aviv, Israel, be moved to Jerusalem, a provocative move which, as expected, angered and alarmed the Palestinians whose land was stolen from them by the UN, the British and America in 1947 and 1948, under false pretenses.

Later, in 2019, Trump endorsed the permanent annexation of the Golan Heights seized in 1967 by the rogue terrorist Israeli state from Syria. This is the same Israeli state which had a heavy hand in perpetrating the false flag attack of 9/11 in concert with the CIA and top officials in the U.S. government and the mainstream media they own and control to launch the unending war on terror. For anyone to suggest that Trump did not know of these Zionist schemes and atrocities is beyond naive.

In 2017, in response to two chemical weapons false flag attacks in Syria, Trump ordered the firing of 62 cruise missiles directed at Syrian military targets which appeared to have been largely vacated. This unwarranted and unprovoked action by Trump provided cover for Israel's continuing air strikes against Syrian targets to destabilize that nation in furtherance of Israel's designs for its Greater Israel Project.

In early 2020, Trump ordered the assassination of Iranian General Qasem Soleimani in a highly provocative move on Trump's part, after having unilaterally withdrawn from the Joint Comprehensive Plan of Action (JCPOA) nuclear deal with Iran in May of 2018. Both actions served to advance the agenda of corrupt Israeli Prime Minister Benjamin Netanyahu, who has been working tirelessly to try to drag the United States into a confrontation with Iran which would only serve to strengthen Israel's strategic position in the Middle East. It hardly takes a rocket scientist to figure out who is calling the shots here and Trump clearly wasn't it. Moreover, Joe Biden is in no different a position as Trump was with respect to the Zionists.

Trump proposed, promoted and pushed through record-setting annual budgets for the Department of Defense (DOD), which served to enrich his Jewish Wall Street bankster friends who were and who remain heavily invested in the military-industrial-surveillance complex and industry. This was in spite of the fact that America's military spending equals that of the next eight largest nations in terms of military spending combined. Thus, the endless saber-rattling and calls of alarm over Chinese, Russian, Iranian and North Korean military threats that we see promoted by the lying mainstream media are merely the endless fear-mongering that the military establishment engages in year after year to feed the corrupt money machine of the military industrial complex. Simply put, retired Marine Major General Smedley Butler, two-time winner of the Congressional Medal of Honor for bravery, was right when he claimed in his 1930s booklet that *War is a Racket.* It was true then, and it remains no less true today, and Donald Trump perpetuated that con during his time in office.

During Trump's watch he called for the creation of the Space Force at a time in which many Americans, including myself, have become distinctly aware that effectively there is no such thing as space and that NASA's alleged moon landings were all faked and staged by Stanley Kubrick and his film crews in the Nevada desert at night to deceive the masses of America and the world. It was all fake and yet another distraction and diversion from the truth that we live on a round, flat, stationary earth with a dome (firmament) over it, inside of which revolve the sun and moon in a clockwise direction, when viewed from above.

6. Clues that Trump is a Card-Carrying Swamp Rat Just Like all the Rest

In response to the Parkland, Florida (Stoneman Douglas High School) false flag attack in early 2018, Trump supported "red flag" gun confiscation laws which seek to legalize the seizure of firearms by permitting police or family members to petition a court to order the removal of firearms from a person who such persons claim (many times falsely) may be a danger to themselves or to others. During his Presidential campaign, Trump promised that he would protect and defend the second amendment which asserts that "the right of the people to keep and bear Arms, shall not be infringed." [31] So Trump lied to the American people and he violated his oath of office at his inauguration by failing to fully protect and defend the Constitution of the United States.

During the Covid scare and scam of 2020, Trump allowed con artist Anthony Fauci a totalitarian platform to spew lies and promote public health policies which were criminally negligent and destructive to Americans' health and livelihoods in the form of face mask, social distancing, sanitation and lockdown mandates. Trump had every opportunity to use his bully pulpit to put an immediate halt to what has proven to be the most effective and harmful global psyop ever to be perpetrated upon mankind in all of world history, by exposing it for what it so clearly is. Trump did none of that. In fact, he ordered Operation Warp Speed to accelerate the development and clinical trials of experimental vaccines that have been rushed to market without the usual Phase 2 animal study trials because of the artificially induced public panic that they themselves deliberately created to sell billions of dollars of unproven, unwarranted vaccines for a contagion that does not warrant the label of "pandemic," whose lethality, according to the CDC, is 0.24%, which is comparable to the mortality rate for the annual flu, for which no such extreme public health measures have ever been employed. In effect, Trump served as Big Pharma's top salesman in promoting an unproven and potentially unsafe vaccine for a health condition that does not warrant such

[31] *The Constitution of the United States.* National Center for Constitutional Studies, 2009. p. 21.

aggressive measures when proven treatments with a high success rate exist, but are often concealed from the public for nefarious reasons. When the dust eventually settles on the Covid scamdemic and the truth comes out, mankind will learn that the unwarranted and reckless public health measures in response to a relatively harmless problem will go down as one of the greatest crimes against humanity ever perpetrated upon mankind. And Donald Trump is as guilty as any of the other co-conspirators in this nefarious plot to enslave and harm humanity.

Lastly, in the face of overwhelming evidence that the Presidential election of November 3, 2020 was fraudulent and that Trump may even have won with as much as 75% of the popular vote, Americans who voted for Trump were disenfranchised and their votes negated by a universally corrupt, fraudulent and dishonest system. In response to this overwhelming evidence, either Trump was all alone and treacherously betrayed by his own Republican Party, his White House staff, the federal judiciary, the lying mainstream media, the FBI, DOJ and the U.S. military, or he knowingly and purposefully went along with the crime to steal America from the American citizens in a silent Jewish New World Order coup of the utmost corruption and wickedness.

When you combine all the clues of what it would have taken to expose the full depths of the global conspiracy and to decisively unseat and defeat it, that Trump did not do, along with the many sins of commission which Trump is clearly guilty of, only a blind fool and a hopelessly wishful thinker could ever view Donald Trump as the hero and savior of the United States that so many of his support base unthinkingly hoped he would prove to be. The simple truth is that no one, no matter how noble, righteous and competent, could have ever unseated the globalist political and economic beast system of Revelation 13:1-10 which rules our world today now wide out in the open for all to see. Donald Trump was merely a man, and a very flawed one at that, whose actions, while in office and over his lifetime, revealed him to be a man characterized by arrogance, egomania, narcissism, dishonesty and moral depravity that should have been easily identified by any man of God indwelled by God's Holy Spirit. Sadly, there are very few such Americans left in 2021 to be able to see what should be so obvious to all of us. As a nation, America is a country of morally depraved and wicked fools, many of whom still remain self-deceived that there is anything good in any of them:

> *"The heart is deceitful above all things, and desperately wicked: who can know it?"* Jeremiah 17:9
>
> *"As it is written, There is none righteous, no, not one: There is none that understandeth, there is none that seeketh after God (Eloah). They are all gone out of the way, they are together become unprofitable; there is none that doeth good, no, not one."* Romans 3:10-12

Today, criminal Joe Biden sits in the White House making a mockery of America and all the values it once claimed it stood for. Donald Trump is gone. He failed his support base, as it was inevitable that he would do. America and the world are reduced to submitting and surrendering their lives and their wills to YHWH, the almighty God of the KJV Bible, and doing things His way, or perishing in their many sins. The choice could not be more obvious. YHWH (God) will step in rather suddenly and quite soon. When He does, will He find you still wanting, still playing pretend that all is fine, when nothing really is? Or will He find you seeking and begging for His mercy, as He will find me? Only time will tell.

7. Final Thoughts

Today is February 10, 2021, three weeks after Joe Biden and Kamala Harris were fraudulently sworn in as the latest Puppet-in-Chief and Vice Puppet-in-Chief of what once purported to be a legitimate constitutional republic and the leader of the free world. Today, the entire world can clearly see that the United States is a godless, deceitful, fraudulent, corrupt, decadent and dead former empire. Its motto of "In God We Trust" is a blatant and monstrous lie that makes a mockery out of God, the Bible and the objective, absolute and universal truth. Those posing as our new leaders today define what the *Protocols of the Learned Elders of Zionism* promised us would happen, because they would make it happen:

> "For a time, until there will no longer be any risk in entrusting responsible posts in our States to our brother-Jews, we shall put them in the hands of persons whose past and reputation are such that between them and the people lies an abyss, persons who, in case of disobedience to our instructions, must face criminals charges or disappear - this in order to make them defend our interests to their last gasp." [32]

Thus, as of this writing, it appears that the globalist beast system of Revelation 13:1-10 has won and that Trump and Q Anon have been proven to be irrelevant. And yet, according to YHWH, the God of the Bible, this story is not yet over; not by a long shot. The way the story ends, Yahushua (Christ) returns to gather the elect (first the dead and then the living) to Himself

---

[32] *Protocols of the Meetings of the Learned Elders of Zion.* Protocol No. 8, last paragraph, p. 25.

in the clouds, and then returns with His army of resurrected saints in tow to destroy all the wicked once and for all and to usher in a new heaven and new earth wherein dwelleth righteousness.

With the benefit of hindsight, and from the many clues of inaction which both Trump and Q Anon manifested over the past three plus years, critically thinking observers can fairly easily deduce that Q Anon was a clever and sophisticated military intelligence psyop that was designed to divert the attention of Americans who view themselves as patriots, conservatives and Christians from the great steal. The authors of the Q Anon psyop dropped enough clues pointing to the realities of the deep state global elite conspiracy of pedophiles and Satanists that their fans failed to factor into their thinking that there were clues all along that something was not right about the whole thing.

It started with Q Anon's very first post with which I opened this book that made claims that Hillary Clinton was facing imminent arrest for a variety of unidentified criminal actions. From all appearances, that prediction was never realized. Anyone with substantive executive business management and leadership experience as I have, knows that anyone who over-commits and under-delivers on promised actions is a con artist and a fraud who should never again be trusted. And yet, in our world and nation, where have you ever witnessed such competence and integrity? Tragically, most Americans never have. So most Americans are reduced to trusting in no one or putting their faith in charlatans, con artists and frauds. It gave Q Anon the perfect opening to take advantage of a large number of naive and gullible American patriots, political conservatives and fools who were desperate for a hero of any kind and willing to overlook the many warning signs that Q Anon was not a reliable and trustworthy source of information.

During Q Anon's run, those of us who monitored the Q posts repeatedly witnessed Q urging their followers to trust the plan, trust Sessions, trust Wray, and trust Huber. In today's world of almost universal deceit, trusting anyone, especially an entity whose real identity is murky and unknown, is the height of folly. A wise man knows not to trust anyone but God, because almost everyone else is a liar and a con artist. Until a person acquires this wisdom of the ages, he will be forever blown about by the winds of unsubstantiated claims that seldom, if ever, are realized. These are the circumstances of the over three year psyop of Q Anon, and anyone foolish enough to get swept up in the hype, is not someone whose judgment and moral integrity can or should ever be trusted.

It is instructive to note that Q's latest post, Post #4953, was made on December 8, 2020, over two months ago. It provided a link to a YouTube video, which has since been taken down, entitled, "We're Not Gonna Take It." So it appears that those behind the Q Anon psyop were intent on fomenting conflict and anger among their patriot followers. Anger and conflict incited in such a manner provides a pretext and an excuse for the invoking of greater government tyranny and martial law, which is what the globalist cabal clearly wants.

Toward the end of Trump's Presidency, Q Anon's posts diminished in their frequency and in the useful clues that they offered those following them. If Q Anon were being employed as an ongoing communications tool to marshal support for a movement of any kind among Trump's support base, this would have never been allowed to happen. The events surrounding the horrendous voter and election fraud of November 3, 2020 begged for daily progress updates of what was being done to oppose the election theft; and yet, there was almost nothing posted by Q over it. In recent months, we witnessed Amazon and the major social media platforms banning the sale of all Q related merchandise and removing any social media content or accounts which mentioned the Q movement. What did that accomplish and what was its obvious intent? Again, it was to foment anger and conflict within the Q movement directed at the political left in this country, in the hopes that it might result in a violent response of some sort that might serve as the excuse to impose harsher measures of government tyranny upon the public, up to and including the imposition of martial law.

Furthermore, Q Anon employed several slogans and ideas that upon closer examination reveal a real lack of genuine insight and an attempt to let their readers draw into Q's statements whatever conclusions they chose to attribute to those vague, non-specific slogans One example of this is found in Q Post #4951, dated November 12, 2020 in which Q stated, "Nothing Can Stop What Is Coming." That's true. But what is coming? Q never made any firm prediction of what that might be. Moreover, what does the often repeated slogan, "Where We Go One, We Go All" or WWG1WGA really mean in a society and nation that is sharply divided, and in which everything the American people believe is false? How is unity achieved under such circumstances? It never can be. So Q's readers are left to draw whatever images they choose to conjure up of what this might look like to them that is likely to sharply differ with what others may imagine it to means to them.

Finally, Q repeatedly asserted that to wake up the American public to what was really going on behind the scenes, they would need to witness certain public events for themselves, such as the extent and nature of the voting and election fraud and theft of November 3, 2020. But is that true? Did it make any difference to the ultimate outcome? No, it did not. The great awakening that many American patriots hoped for is a pipe dream. Furthermore, it will never happen. The Bible explains why in 2 Thessalonians 2:10-12. God has sent strong delusion upon the masses, so that they will believe a lie and be damned, for having rejected the truth, and taken pleasure in unrighteousness. Q Post #4951 concludes with the line, "Sometimes you must walk through the darkness before you see light." That too is true. But sometimes, and this is one of those times, the majority of the public will never see the light and will be forever in darkness. Thus, Q Anon told their intended audience what they wanted to and so desperately hoped to hear. It wasn't the truth, yet again.

The bigger question for all of us ought to be, now what? The benefits of hindsight have now confirmed what the Bible's wisdom of the ages has been teaching us all along:

> *"It is better to trust in the LORD (YHWH) than to put confidence in man. It is better to trust in the LORD (YHWH) than to put confidence in princes."* Psalm 118:8-9

> *"Put not your trust in princes, nor in the son of man, in whom there is no help. His breath goeth forth, he returneth to the earth; in that day his very thoughts perish. Happy is he that hath the God (Eloah) of Jacob for his help, whose hope is in the LORD (YHWH) his God (Elohim):"* Psalm 146:3-5

> *"There is a way which seemeth right unto a man, but the end thereof are the ways of death."* Proverbs 14:12

> *"Trust in the LORD (YHWH) with all thine heart; and lean not unto thine own understanding. In all thy ways acknowledge him, and he shall direct thy paths. Be not wise in thine own eyes: fear the LORD (YHWH), and depart from evil."* Proverbs 3:5-7

Because most Americans have long ago dismissed God (YHWH) as being irrelevant in their lives and ceased reading, meditating upon and obeying the wisdom and precepts of the Bible, this advice and counsel seems foreign and woefully foolish to most people alive today. Moreover, it serves as the perfect preconditions necessary to mislead and fool an entire nation and the world. If you have failed to invest your life in pursuing the absolute truth and the wisdom of the ages, you are reduced to depending upon your own intuition and insights; and as we have seen above in Proverbs 14:12, such an approach to dealing with life inevitably leads to despair, pain and ultimately, death: both physical and spiritual death. It's what distinguishes the wise and godly sage from the naive and gullible neophyte who fancies himself to be the modern day detective and Sherlock Holmes, but who is neither.

The simple truth is that the world is a very dangerous place and it is the rare person who has an older and wiser mentor or family member teach him this truth. So most of us go through life fairly oblivious to what is really going on underneath the superficial surface of life for decades. Most of us never really wake up and fully get it. I am one of the blessed few who has. But it took me over half a century of living before God Himself began to reveal the deeper truths of the reality of life to me. At first, it was highly disorienting. But I pressed on because I was being driven by powerful spiritual forces I could not see and did not fully understand. I was hungry for knowledge and wisdom and was willing to do whatever it took to attain such insights, because by age 46 I knew I was a fool and I was bound and determined not to remain that way. I had always been at the top of any class I was a part of, and at age 46, I discovered how little I really knew; and I hated that! So I made a vow to myself then to figure out what some other men I met back then already knew. I vowed to become wise. Never in my wildest dreams did I ever imagine it would bring me to this place. But it has. Because God was orchestrating everything for this end.

I am blessed to be one of the most intelligent and insightful people I have ever known. I did nothing to earn this. It was a gift that God chose to bless me with for His greater purposes. I have always longed to be a virtuous, noble and honorable leader and hero. I have always hungered for the truth and had a tender, caring and protective heart for others. I didn't choose any of this. God chose to bless me with these gifts so that I could bless and teach others, once I had figured out some very important things for myself. Here is what I have discovered and learned:

1. God is very real and precisely who He says He is. He created everything by speaking it into existence out of nothing. He is separate from and greater than His entire creation put together. So trying to oppose God is the height of folly. It cannot be done. He has the power to throw any of us into the burning lake of fire and brimstone any time He chooses. The fact that He has not done so for all of us already is a divine miracle and evidence of God's amazingly merciful character. That's why I genuinely fear Him. He gave me a premonition of the burning lake of fire and brimstone 20 years ago that literally scared the hell out of me. It has changed me profoundly and forever. I will never be the same.

2. I don't have a rebellious spirit. I have a spirit that seeks to become wise. So knowing that God is worthy of my fear, I have sought to learn how not to anger Him. Over time, as I came to know and love Him for who He is, I have become devoted to pleasing my heavenly Father to express my devotion to and love for Him. His word, the Bible, which He created for His people to learn how to live well and wisely, tells all of us who are of the truth to do all His commandments, because they are there to protect us from harm. In fact, King Solomon, the wisest man who ever lived (other than Yahushua the Messiah), concluded that the way to live life wisely was to *"fear God and keep all His commandments, for this is the whole duty of man"* in Ecclesiastes 12:13. What was good enough for Solomon, is good enough for me. So I just do it. I don't argue or try to cut corners with an all-knowing God. I'd never get away with it long-term, even if I tried. So I never try. I simply obey because I long to please Him.

3. To keep all God's commandments requires that I read the Bible from cover to cover and know what it says and do all of it. That is why I read 6 chapters from the Bible almost every day. I am now on my eighth full read of the Bible from cover to cover. And to this day, I am still finding new things I had not picked up on in my first seven readings of the Bible. But I do even more than this because I long to be as wise and as close to God as I can become. Thus, I read the first or last 75 Psalms of the Book of Psalms every sabbath day (Saturday) which are prayers that remind me of who God is and all of His merciful promises He makes to those of us who belong completely to Him. I have been doing this since the summer of 2015. I also read one chapter every night whose chapter number corresponds to the date of the month from the Book of Proverbs, the book of wisdom, and I reflect on what I read. I have been doing this since September of 2008. So I have been adhering to this practice for the last 12 and a half years. I also read a page from a daily

devotional authored by Walter A. Henrichsen entitled, *Thoughts from the Diary of a Desperate Man.* Walt was one of the first men from whom I learned about God and the Bible and he has a way of challenging the thoughts and minds of his readers. And finally I talk to God multiple times a day in prayer. These are the practices I follow which allow me to enjoy a direct, personal and intimate relationship with my heavenly Father who has never let me down. Almost everyone in my life has let me down, so the contrast is rather striking and profound for me.

4. As a result of these practices and way of thinking, God inspires my writing and every one of my thoughts in accordance with His will and with His predestinated plan for my life. He doesn't do this with everyone, but this is the rather unusual and unique way in which He interacts with and blesses me. I am distinctly aware of this in my writing, because I never outline anything before I begin writing. I just sit at my keyboard and God takes over and begins inspiring what He wills for me to write. I am simply an empty and submitted vessel, fully devoted to doing His will and delighting Him. I would submit to you, my readers, that were it not for my hunger for wisdom and the practices I have just shared with you here, I would not have possessed the insights into men's characters which has allowed me to see and understand the intrinsic flaws in the Q Anon psyop and the very real character flaws in Donald J. Trump.

Trump was never destined by God to save America from itself, although many self-deceived and self-professing Christians have thought and claimed just this. Now, with the benefit of 20/20 hindsight, we can see that Trump, while a skillful self-promoter and con man, has been just the most recent in a long string of deeply flawed and compromised men who have functioned as the chief puppets of the Jewish synagogue of Satan of Revelation 2:9 and 3:9, the so-called "Learned Elders of Zion," who have schemed for centuries on how to take over the world and rule it behind the scenes with their Orwellian vision of a New World Order global surveillance police state, in which all of us non-Jews are either exterminated or turned into their obedient slaves. This is the ultimate manifestation of the metaphorical economic and political beast system of Revelation 13:1-10 of end times Bible prophecy. The only reason that most humans alive today cannot see this horror for what it so clearly is is because God has blinded them to this greater reality which is now staring all of us in the face. While much of this is due to occult magic spells which have been cast upon the masses by the warlocks and witches of orthodox Judaism and the Zohar Kabbalah, even more today, it is a direct result of God having sent strong delusion upon them, so that they believe a lie and are damned, for having rejected the truth and taken pleasure in unrighteousness as revealed in 2 Thessalonians 2:10-12:

> *"And with all deceivableness of unrighteousness in them that perish;* ***because they received not the love of the truth, that they might be saved. And for this cause God shall send them strong delusion, that they should believe a lie; That they all might be damned*** *who believed not the truth, but had pleasure in unrighteousness.* (Bold face added for emphasis)

Now that Trump's apparent role as savior of the world and of America has been demolished (by God), there are no human agents left that mankind can pin their hopes on. So we all are reduced to trusting God to rescue the few of us, or perish in a New World Order from hell that is entirely of the devil, the father of lies and the destroyer. Stripped from all other options, everyone alive on earth today is now being tested, tried and proven by God to either be a lover or a hater of God and of the truth He embodies with integrity and His awesome power and might.

As of this writing, Joe Biden, Kamala Harris and their ilk are gloating with glee over their apparent victory over the good, the righteous and the godly. Very soon, we can be confident that the sovereign God of the universe will suddenly, and without warning, overthrow the tables of the Jewish money changers for a third and final time and cast all the wicked and foolish of this perishing earth into the lake which burns with fire and brimstone, which they all so richly deserve.

So the bigger story was never about Trump or Q Anon. It was always about God, the mighty and great I AM. Now we wait and watch what God will do with this mess that He, and He alone has orchestrated and predestinated since before the world began, so that in the end, He gets all the glory, honor and praise for His finally destroying evil and bringing true justice once and for all to all of mankind. For those of us on God's side, it is going to be glorious. For those opposing Him, it is inevitably going to be abject terror. And true justice will be done. Praise Yahuwah for that, which is what Hallelujah means.

Bibliography

Allen, Gary. *None Dare Call It Conspiracy.* Buccaneer Books, Cutchogue, NY, 1971. ISBN-13: 978-0-8996617.

Balacius, Robert Alan. *Uncovering the Mysteries of Your Hidden Inheritance.* Sacred Truth Ministries, Mountain City, TN, 2001. ISBN: 1-58840-021-2.

Bennett, Todd D. *Names: The Father, the Son and the Importance of Names in Scriptures.* Shema Yisrael Publications, New York, NY, 2006. ISBN: 0-9768659-2-0.

Benson, Bill and Beckman, M.J. "Red." *The Law That Never Was – The fraud of the 16th Amendment and personal Income Tax.* M.J. "Red" Beckman, Carrolls, WA, 1985.

Clèraubat, Brian Alois. *A Greater "Miracle" Than The Ten Lost Tribes Discovered . . . – The Dead "SIX MILLION" Uncovered . . . !* Institute for Historical Accuracy and Veracity, Mountain City, TN, 2007. ISBN: 1-58840-070-0.

Dubay, Eric. *The Flat-Earth Conspiracy.* 2014. ISBN: 978-1-312-62716-1.

Epperson, Ralph A. *The Unseen Hand: an Introduction to the Conspiratorial View of History.* Publius Press, Tucson, AZ, 1985. ISBN: 978-0-9614135-0-7.

Federer, William J. *America's God and Country Encyclopedia of Quotations.* Amerisearch, Inc., St. Louis, MO, 2000. ISBN: 1-880563-09-6.

Hall, Marshall. *The Earth is Not Moving.* Fair Education Foundation, Inc., Cornelia, GA, 1991. ISBN: 0-932766-20-x.

Henrichsen, Walter A. *Thoughts from the Diary of a Desperate Man.* Leadership Foundation, El Cajon, CA, 1999. ISBN: 0-9704374-2-0.

Hendrie, Edward. *9/11 Enemies Foreign and Domestic: Secret Evidence Censored from the Official Record Proves Traitors Aided Israel in Attacking the USA.* Great Mountain Publishing, Garrisonville, VA, 2010. ISBN: 978-0-9832627-3-2.

Hendrie, Edward. *The Greatest Lie on Earth: Proof That Our World Is Not a Moving Globe.* Great Mountain Publishing, Garrisonville, VA, 2016. ISBN: 978-1-943056-01-9.

Huggins, Hal A., DDS, MS. *Client Education Packet.* Huggins Applied Healing, Colorado Springs, CO, 2012.

https://www.brainyquote.com/quotes/franklin_d_roosevelt_164126

https://www.brainyquote.com/quotes/joseph_stalin_109571

https://www.businessinsider.com/these-6-corporations-control-90-of-the-media-in-america-2012-6.

https://cognitive-liberty.online/j-edgar-hoover-on-monstrous-conspiracy-and-morality/

http://dosmosis.blogspot.com/2011/05/quote-woodrow-wilson-secret-societies.html

https://en.wikiquote.org/wiki/Franklin_D._Roosevelt

https://www.goodreads.com/quotes/tag/secret-societies

https://www.google.com/search?q=benjamin+disraeli+quotes&tbm=isch&source=iu&ictx=1&fir=sUkkTNdIP4V8yM%253A%252CyyfxXHm2-Ly6cM%252C_&vet=1&usg=AI4_-kRfaFzeAberREgCEbV2CcC23sChTA&sa=X&ved=2ahUKEwiiqpbVxOnhAhXHJzQIHTcxA_EQ9QEwBnoECAoQBg#imgrc=sUkkTNdIP4V8yM:

https://www.jfklibrary.org/archives/other-resources/john-f-kennedy-speeches/american-newspaper-publishers-9association-19610427

https://www.nationllibertyalliane.org/two-us-constitutions.

https://nomadicpolitics.blogspot.com/2014/04/nyt-editor-john-swinton-and-truth-about.html

https://opengov.ideascale.com/a/dtd/David-Rockefeller-s-book-Memoirs-admits-secretly-conspiring-for-a-NWO/4007-4049

https://paloaltoonline.com/square/2006/07/04/read-these-nwo-quotes-from-the-real-enemies-of-the-usa

https://www.qanon.pub.

https://www.youtube.com/watch?v=U0kNwvZm_9Q

Koestler, Arthur. *The Thirteenth Tribe.* Pan Books Ltd., London, UK, 1976. ISBN: 0-330-25069-8.

Marrs, Texe. *DNA Science and the Jewish Bloodline.* RiverCrest Publishing, Austin, TX, 2013. ISBN: 978-1-930004-81-8.

Pappe, Ilan. *The Ethnic Cleansing of Palestine.* Oneworld Publications Limited, New York, NY, 2006. ISBN: 978-1-85168-555-4.

Piper, Michael Collins. *Final Judgment: The Missing Link in the JFK Assassination Conspiracy, Volumes 1 and 2.* American Free Press, Washington, D.C., 2005. ISBN: 978-1-937787-37-0.

Protocols of the Meetings of the Learned Elders of Zion. Pyramid Book Shop, Houston, TX, 1934 (first published in Russian in 1905). ISBN: 978-1-162935133.

Shannan, Pat. *Everything They* Ever Told Me Was a Lie.* American Free Press, Washington, D.C., 2010. ISBN: 978-0-9823448-5-9.

Skousen, Cleon W. *The Naked Capitalist.* Buccaneer Books, Cutchogue, NY, 1970. ISBN: 0-89968-323-1.

Sussman, Brian. *Climategate.* WorldNetDaily, Washington D.C., 2010. ISBN: 978-1-935071-83-9.

Thorn, Victor. *Made in Israel: 9-11 and the Jewish Plot Against America.* Sisyphus Press, State College, PA 2011. ISBN: 978-1-61364-279-5.

Trump, Mary L., PhD. *Too Much and Never Enough: How my Family Created the World's Most Dangerous Man.* Simon & Schuster, New York, NY, 2020. ISBN: 978-1-9821-4146-2.

Weiland, Ted R. *God's Covenant People: Yesterday, Today and Forever.* Mission to Israel Ministries, Scottsbluff, NE, 1994.

Where We Go One We Go All (various authors). *QAnon: An Invitation to the Great Awakening.* Relentlessly Creative Books, Dallas, TX, 2019. ISBN: 978-1-942790-13-6.

About the Author

David Lionheart is a researcher, author and blogger on the global conspiracy and its many obvious connections to the fulfillment of end times Bible prophecy, what it all means and what we can expect in the very near future.

Prior to his current career, Lionheart was a business management consultant and turnaround Chief Financial Officer (CFO) and general manager for half a dozen smaller high and low tech companies in the San Francisco Bay Area over a 30 year career in a variety of challenging conditions. He was instrumental in the successful turnaround and sale of one of those companies in a mergers & acquisitions transaction and in turning around and taking a second company public in an Initial Public Offering (IPO) and remained as that company's public company CFO for five years thereafter.

Lionheart holds a bachelor's degree in Economics from U.C. Davis with Highest Honors and Phi Beta Kappa and Phi Kappa Phi honors distinctions and an MBA degree from the Harvard Business School with second year honors. As part of his formal education and subsequent research on his own, he has a particular expertise in and understanding of world history, political science, economics, philosophy, psychology, finance, business strategy, organizational behavior, American sociology and biblical theology, all of which were vitally important to the writing of his books.

For More Writings by the Author

David Lionheart has authored the following other ground-breaking books:

> *Making Sense Out of World Gone Mad: A Roadmap for God's Elect Living in the Finals Days of the End Times,* (published in February 2015)
>
> *Spiritual Warfare in the Final Days of the End Times* (published in September 2016)
>
> *Reflections of a Watchman on the Wall in the Final Days of the End Times* (published in October 2016)
>
> *The Final Act of God's Play* (published in January 2021)
>
> *There is NO Virus!* (published in September 2021)

The author has extensively blogged under his Watchman on the Wall moniker on Disqus and maintains his own website and blog at:

www.dlionheart.com.

He also posts extensively under his given name, David Lionheart, on Facebook.

www.ingramcontent.com/pod-product-compliance
Lightning Source LLC
LaVergne TN
LVHW010937110826
845149LV00013B/2633
9780998382524